Alexander Walker

**Mary, Queen of Scots**

A narrative and defence

Alexander Walker

**Mary, Queen of Scots**
*A narrative and defence*

ISBN/EAN: 9783337324193

Printed in Europe, USA, Canada, Australia, Japan

Cover: Foto ©ninafisch / pixelio.de

More available books at **www.hansebooks.com**

# MARY
# QUEEN OF SCOTS

*A NARRATIVE AND DEFENCE*

BY

*AN ELDER OF THE CHURCH OF SCOTLAND*

WITH PORTRAIT AND EIGHT ILLUSTRATIONS

SPECIALLY DRAWN FOR THE WORK

ABERDEEN
THE UNIVERSITY PRESS
1889

TO
THE MEMORY
OF
MARY
MARTYR QUEEN OF SCOTS
THE FOLLOWING PAGES
ARE
𝔇edicated

A Pure Woman, a Faithful Wife, a Sovereign
Enlightened beyond the Tutors
of Her Age

# FOREWORD.

AN effort is made in the few following pages to condense the reading of many years, and the conclusion drawn from almost all that has been written in defence and in defame of Mary Stuart.

Long ago the world was at one as to the character of the Casket Letters. To these forgeries the writer thinks there must now be added that document discovered in the Charter Room of Dunrobin Castle by Dr. John Stuart.

In that most important and deeply interesting find, recently made in a loft above the princely stables of Belvoir Castle, in a letter from Randolph to Rutland, of 10th June, 1563, these words occur in writing about our Queen: "She is the fynneste she that ever was". This deliberately expressed opinion of Thomas Randolph will, I hope, be the opinion of my readers.

The Author has neither loaded his page with long footnote extracts, nor enlarged his volume with ponderous glossarial or other appendices.

To the pencil of Mr. J. G. Murray of Aberdeen, and the etching needle of M. Vaucanu of Paris, the little book is much beholden.

A. W.

64 HAMILTON PLACE,
ABERDEEN.

# CONTENTS.

|  | PAGE |
|---|---|
| FOREWORD, . . . . . | v |

### CHAPTER I.
HER BIRTH AND CHILDHOOD, . . . . . 1

### CHAPTER II.
THE PROGRESS OF HER EDUCATION, . . . 6

### CHAPTER III.
SHE TAKES POSSESSION OF HER FATHER'S THRONE, . . . 10

### CHAPTER IV.
RICCIO MURDERED; MORAY SUDDENLY RE-ENTERS EDINBURGH, . . 21

### CHAPTER V.
KING HENRY THREATENS TO GO ABROAD, . . 25

### CHAPTER VI.
THE LIEUTENANT OF THE MARCHES CANNOT KEEP THE ASSIZE, . 32

### CHAPTER VII.
MARY LITTLE DREAMS OF THE CALAMITY ABOUT TO FALL UPON HER, 44

### CHAPTER VIII.
MARY TREMBLES FOR THE SAFETY OF HER CHILD, . . . 69

### CHAPTER IX.
THE DOUBLE PROCESS OF DIVORCE. . . 82

## CHAPTER X.
JOHN CRAIG AND THE BANNS, . . . 94

## CHAPTER XI.
THE WOFUL WEDDING, . . . 99

## CHAPTER XII.
NOT HOLYROOD, BUT LOCHLEVEN, . . . 109

## CHAPTER XIII.
THE SILVER CASKET, . . . . 116

## CHAPTER XIV.
QUEEN ONCE MORE, . . . . 127

## CHAPTER XV.
INTO ENGLAND, . . . . 130

## CHAPTER XVI.
THE END APPROACHES, . . . . 147

## CHAPTER XVII.
THE TROUBLOUS PILGRIMAGE ENDS, . . 158

## ILLUSTRATIONS.

Etched Portrait of Mary Stuart.

The Castlegate of Aberdeen.

Palace of Linlithgow.

Mary's Room in Holyrood.

Stirling Castle.

Lochleven Castle.

Cathcart Castle.

Dundrennan Abbey.

The Wild Ride by Night.

# MARY QUEEN OF SCOTS.

## Chapter I.

### Her Birth and Childhood.

> There beats no heart on either border,
> Where through the north blasts blow,
> But keeps your memory as a warder
> His beacon fire aglow.
> —SWINBURNE.

ALL Scotsmen and Scotswomen know that when Mary's father, James the Fifth, "King of the Commons," heard of her birth, as he lay sick unto death in Falkland Palace, he said: "Well, well, the croun cam' wi' a lass, and will gang wi' a lass". Mary, born on the 8th day of December, 1542, was six days old when her father died. Her mother, James the Fifth's second wife, Dowager-Duchess of Longueville, daughter of Claude of Lorraine, Duke of Guise, and of Antoinette de Bourbon, was a lady of the most illustrious descent in Europe, and in every way qualified to reign. Mary was the prettiest baby of royal race in Europe, and became the most important person on the whole chess-board of European politics; and before she was many months old, English, French, and Scottish blood was shed in rivalry for her tiny hand. So early as March, 1543, the charge of the child's personal safety was entrusted by the Parliament to Lords Erskine and Livingstone, as Commissioners, bound to fidelity under pain of loss of life, land, and goods, and her nursing was confided to the Queen-Mother.

With a truculent and unscrupulous neighbour like Henry VIII., even with two powerful nobles for her guardians, the infant Queen was not considered to be altogether safe in the Palace of Linlithgow. She was accordingly removed to Stirling, and that without the assent of the Governor, for we find Parliament, in December, 1543, indemnifying those who had convened for removing the Queen from Linlithgow to Stirling; it appears, however, that her household was not finally installed in Stirling till 1545. Before she left Linlithgow, Chalmers infers from "Sadler's State Letters" that Mary had the smallpox; but this disorder does not seem to have impaired her beauty, otherwise we should probably have had some mention of this circumstance by one or other of the many writers who have left us descriptions of her person.

She remained for two years and a half at Stirling Castle under the eye of the Queen-Mother, attended by her nurse, Janet Sinclair, whose faithful care was rewarded by repeated grants from Parliament. Mary, when she came of age, granted Janet's husband, John Kemp, a pension of money and victual. The Lady Fleming, a natural daughter of James IV., was also in attendance as governess. The Queen-Mother, in order to insure emulation in Mary's studies, judiciously chose for her four playmates of the same age. Four Maries were probably selected to wait upon Mary their Queen because there are four mentioned in the Gospels as frequently in company with the Mother of our Redeemer. From very early times disputes about the individuality of these saintly women have existed among Christians; but we may take—(1) Mary, mother of James and John, (2) Mary of Cleophas, (3) Mary, the mother of Mark, and (4) Mary Magdalene. People in those times knew the Bible better than they get credit for. These children were all from families of rank: Mary Beaton was the well-known Cardinal's niece; Mary Seton was the daughter of

Lord Seton; Mary Fleming was the daughter of Lord Fleming, whose mother was the Queen's governess; and Mary Livingstone was the daughter of Lord Livingstone, one of the Commissioners who had charge of the Queen's person.

The defeat at Pinkie on the 10th September, 1547, did not lessen the dislike of the Scots to the rude English wooing of their sovereign. They decided to accept the alliance with France, and at six years of age Mary was placed on board one of the four French galleys which Villegagnon had brought from Leith to Dumbarton through the Pentland Frith. An English fleet watched in vain to intercept the little squadron. The peasants of Bretagne show the spot where, on the 13th of August, 1548, a Queen of Scotland and of France first stepped on their sunny shore at Roscoff, after safely evading the sinister designs of England. A chapel dedicated to St. Ninian, the apostle of Galloway, still shows her gratitude and that of her friends for her safety—though, to Scotland's shame, it has been for several years threatened with ruin. Received with every attention due to her queenly rank at St. Germain-en-Laye, the little maiden who already filled the ancient Scottish throne was in legal form betrothed to the Dauphin of France, eldest son of Henry II.

and Catharine de Medici. But the shadow of her grandeur stretched itself already dark and deep by her side. By some fatal chance or choice, her half-brother, James, then a stripling of seventeen years of age—one of her father's too numerous illegitimate children—had sailed with her from the Clyde. He thus early secured her sisterly affection and an elder brother's influence on that sister's warm heart.

## Chapter II.

### The Progress of Her Education.

But fairer far than all the crowd who bask on fortune's tide,
Effulgent in the light of youth, is she, the new made bride ;
The homage of a thousand hearts—the fond deep love of one—
The hopes that dance around a life whose charms are but begun.
—BELL.

YOUNG though she was when taken from her Northern home, Mary Stuart had received careful and efficient instruction from John Erskine, Prior of Inchmahoume, and Alexander Scott, Parson of Balmaclellan. During the ten years which followed her landing in France, she was brought up under the care of her maternal grandmother, often seeing, as duty enjoined, the sisters and kinswomen of her betrothed. Neither frivolous nor superficial was the influence on our young Queen of such a relation, who was "humble, devout, and charitable, and conducted [her husband's] house liker to a monastery than the court of a great prince". Her maternal uncles naturally watched with anxiety the development of her character and disposition. Both Duke and Cardinal are said to have early attracted her confidence and to have never lost it. When her grandfather, Duke Claude, died, on the 12th of April, 1550, Mary took part in the funeral ceremonies and shared the sorrows of the illustrious house to which she was so closely allied.

Eight days after this event, peace was proclaimed at the cross of Edinburgh; the seas were so far freed from danger; and Mary's mother resolved to visit her. The Queen-Dowager of Scotland, mother of the gifted and beautiful girl, the affianced bride of their future King, reached Dieppe on the 19th September, 1550, and was received by the French people and Court at Rouen with every possible mark of respect. Another well-loved object called Mary of Lorraine to the home of her kindred. While her royal daughter had for two years been removed from her influence, for twelve long and trying years she had not seen her son Francis, Duke of Longueville. She found great reason to be proud of both her children, but ere long a double sorrow came to wound her heart. On the 22nd September, 1551, her son was taken from her by death—he who might have proved a stay and protector to his little sister in the days of need that were at hand. About the same time a frustrated attempt to poison her daughter was made public.

After a stay of fourteen months in France, the Queen-Dowager returned to Scotland with a heavy load of sorrow, in November, 1551. Had she foreseen what anxiety and affliction the government of a half-civilised nation, swayed at will by a restless and selfish oligarchy, was to bring to her during the next eight and a half years, she would probably never have returned. On the 24th of April, 1558, with much pomp, Mary Stuart was married to the Dauphin, on a splendid platform erected in front of the Church of Notre Dame at Paris. On the 10th of July, 1559, the death of Henry the Second gave the crown of France to her husband, who assumed the title of Francis II. The long series of Mary's misfortunes began on the 8th of December, 1560, when her husband died. Had her character had time to unfold itself, had her talents been as precocious as her beauty, Mary Stuart might then with a little ambition have seized a sceptre more powerful than any which had ever fallen to a sovereign of the Scots. The reins of the government of France, on account of her extreme youth, fell into the hands of her mother-in-law, Catharine de Medici. In some moment of curiosity and forgetfulness, Mary is said to have asked whether her mother-in-law was not the daughter of a merchant of Florence. The hasty phrase was not relished, nor the unintended sting forgotten, when Mary Stuart, herself also a Queen-Dowager, and yet almost a child, had to stand beside the haughty Catharine; nor in future years, when Mary's fate depended on Catharine's good or ill will.

The death of Mary's mother on the 10th of June, 1560, left Scotland without a ruler, while convulsed with the throes of the Reformation. Looking back with regret to the happy years of her girlhood, looking with foreboding to the future, Mary had to bid adieu to France, and in four days—some say five, some six—*i.e.*, on 19th August, 1561, she safely landed in Leith, having again escaped the English warships sent to capture her. In that age France was far more advanced than Scotland in everything that constitutes the comfort and grace and dignity of life; and Mary may well be pardoned if, after having adorned by her girlish beauty, her wit and learning, the most splendid Court in Europe, she felt, and showed to others that she felt, the rudeness and poverty of her ancestral realm; but with courage she set herself to the task of government, which she could not shun.

## Chapter III.

### She takes Possession of her Father's Throne.

> Amid her lords and ladies gay,
> Slowly she ambled on her way.
> Priest, abbot, layman, all were there,
> And presbyter with look severe.
> There rode the lords of France and Spain,
> Of England, Flanders, and Lorraine,
> While serried thousands round them stood,
> From shore of Leith to Holyrood.
> —*The Queen's Wake.*

AT the date of the Queen's landing in Scotland Elizabeth had ruled England for about three years. The rare skill and talents of the ministers who offered her their services, the immense interests which bound a numerous and active section of English nobles to the faith she had adopted, strengthened Elizabeth's hands.

Mary Stuart's position was different. Her hands were weakened by the need, the greed, and turbulent character of a majority of her nobles. The New Evangel and English gold had undermined the royal authority and the supremacy of the law. On their estates the nobles ruled their kindred and their inferiors with a mixture of French feudalism and the independence of Gaelic chiefs. The system of bonds and manrents, which James III. and his successors had tried in vain to extinguish, enabled them to combine for the execution of any crime and to deprive the Crown of any power to bring them to punishment. Dearer to Mary than her life or crown was her faith. She had no Cecil, astute though unprincipled, to guide and counsel her. The witchery of her manner, her beauty, and her wit won some of the nobles in a half-hearted way to her side, but it was almost single-handed that Mary, in the nineteenth year of her age, began to rule. Those, indeed, whom circumstances induced her to select as her counsellors proved to be in league and correspondence with the foes of her creed and the liberties of her subjects.

The abolition of the Mass and of the Papal supremacy had, on the 24th August, 1560, received the sanction of a Scottish Parliament, the legality of which was questionable and is still questioned; but Mary was content to leave affairs as she found them, requiring only—as surely a queen had right to require—leave to use her own religion, and to keep unmolested the faith she had inherited. One cannot help feeling that if John Knox had not placed his fanaticism at the disposal of a rapacious faction, and if the daughter of Anne Boleyn had been less fickle in religion and less jealous in temperament, Mary's future life would have been freed from many a tragedy. It is said that Mary rejected the counsel which the Northland barons gave her ere she left France. Their projects were less revolutionary, and John Leslie laid them before her at Vitri, in Champagne, on the 15th of April, 1561. We know that the advisers whom she chose were leaders of the Protestant cause, chief among them being that half-brother who, fourteen years before, had sailed with her from Dumbarton. James Stuart, ambitious, hypocritical, and heartless, gave Mary's progress to the North the proportions of a campaign, and, on the 10th of September, 1562, managed to get himself proclaimed Earl of Moray at Darnaway Castle, and to crush for a time the great house of Huntly.

In the battle at Corrichie—a cleft in the Hill of Fare, in Aberdeenshire—on the 28th October, 1562, the Earl of Huntly was slain, some assert, by Moray's own hand. On the Castlegate of Aberdeen, two days after the fight, five gentlemen of the Clan Gordon were hanged; and three days after that bloody deed, namely,

on the 2nd November, 1562, Huntly's third son, the gallant Sir John, was led forth to execution on a scaffold erected in the Castle-gate; and it is on record that Moray had the brutality to force his half-sister and Queen to a window in the house of Earl Marischal, that she might witness in spite of herself the untimely end of a man whom, popular ballads say, she tenderly loved. On beholding his sovereign the unhappy knight dropped on his knees, and turned his eyes up to her with a steadfast gaze. The cruel spectacle drew a flood of tears from Mary. Such a scene was not for the eyes of a girl not yet twenty. The executioner was unskilful, and the victim did not expire until after many blows.

On the 4th November the Queen went South. By her progress in the North, under the guidance of Moray, she could have gained nothing but a little insight into the character of her relative. His unbridled greed had shown itself at Darnaway as barefaced as that of the band of adherents with whom he had surrounded her. Little had the new faith to be proud of in proselytes like Moray or Lethington, Morton or Glencairn. Toleration for the convictions of others they had none. "They were Protestants," says John Knox, "for their own commoditie". The Church's lands and wealth were temptations too great for baron or burgh. The ministers of the new faith, and a provision for them, formed no part of their programme. The "said John" cried aloud, but his projects were derided as a "devout imagination," and into the pockets of laymen and burghs went the greater part of the patrimony of the Church. Meanwhile Mary kept firmly to the faith in which she had been trained.

The following list of suitors for her hand shows how much her smile was coveted: The King of Sweden, the King of Denmark, the King of France, the Archduke Charles of Austria, Don Carlos of Spain, the Duke of Ferrara, the Duke of Nemours, the Duke of Anjou, the Earl of Arran, and the Earl of Leicester. Mary may have felt flattered by the suit of Don Carlos, heir to what was then the widest empire in the world, yet she married suddenly her own cousin, in spite of many plots. Two years younger than herself, Henry Stuart, Lord Darnley, son of Matthew, Earl of Lennox, and of Margaret Douglas, grand-daughter of King Henry VII., was one of the nearest heirs to the English crown. Beyond this he had nothing but his good looks to recommend him; was weak, needy, insolent, and vicious. He was the tallest man in the

Isle of Britain. If he had any religious belief at all, it was, if we may trust his professions, an unsteady adherence to the old creed. When his self-conceit was wounded, he had occasional fits of zeal, but his religion had little effect on his daily life. Like the Queen, he loved the horse, the hound, the hawk; but he could not, like the Queen, restrain his passion within the limits prescribed by the urgencies of public business. The marriage in Holyrood, on the 29th July, 1565, was the signal for revolt. Mary had, in June, a month before her marriage, in answer to a demand from the General Assembly to adopt measures for the suppression of the Mass and other Catholic practices, said "that she did not believe in the Protestant religion; she saw nothing wrong in the Mass; that she believed the Roman Catholic religion to be well founded; and that, as she had never pressed her Scottish subjects against their consciences to accept a religion, they should not seek to press her; she had not in the past sought to impose her religion on them, and they might in the future worship God as they pleased".

Darnley's dissolute habits and insolent, petulant ways deepened the envy and dislike which the nobles took to him. When Elizabeth permitted the ill-starred young man to visit the Scottish Court, she might have guessed what would happen. Mary's thoughts were turned too often to the English succession, and the idea of strengthening her own and annihilating a rival claim was sure to suggest itself. Yet the marriage made Elizabeth the open foe of her cousin. Moray sneaked away from the Court and plotted to dethrone his sister with Châtellerault, Argyle, Glencairn, Boyd, and all who like them dreaded the restoration of the Lennox family to its power and influence in the western counties. The rebellious band got some money and more encouragement from Elizabeth. They flattered themselves that Mary had lost her popularity, and, getting together near Glasgow an army, they prepared to cross swords with the Queen's loyal supporters. But 5000 horsemen sprang into their saddles to vindicate their sovereign's right to wed the man of her choice; and, placing herself at their head, with Darnley and his father on either hand, she moved to the attack. Her opponents waited not her coming, but fled to Dumfries, intending to wait there for the promised aid from England. They waited in vain. The English Queen showed her sympathy with the insurgents in another and less expensive way. With a woman's petty spite she imprisoned in the Tower Darnley's mother, the Countess of Lennox.

Many weeks had not elapsed when Mary discovered that the character of her young husband was deplorably defective; his total incapacity for business and obstinate intemperance forced her to look for some one to carry on her private correspondence in French with her friends on the Continent. The crowd who filled her Court was a mob of men, proud, quarrelsome, intractable, untrained to steady business and recoiling from the idea of it, filled with mutual malice and hatred, and striving to outdo each other in treachery to their sovereign and their country. The young Queen had been forced in her extremity to turn to an Italian of mean degree, who had come to Edinburgh in the retinue of Moret, the Ambassador of Piedmont, in 1561. David Riccio had acquired abroad some knowledge of the politics of the day, and was beginning to show some discernment of men and things in the Scottish Court. Though no monarch in Christendom was of prouder lineage, Mary Stuart, to her honour, acted on her expressed conviction that lowly birth should not bar the path of merit to promotion—enlightened in this as in other views beyond the tutors of her age. Her marriage brought her no such alleviation of her labours and difficulties as she had a right to expect; finding them rather increased, she had no resource but to depend still more on the services of this talented foreigner. In the *Melville Memoirs* we have a graphic description of the rude and savage handling the secretary had from the Protestant nobles. Darnley turned fiercely against the man to whom he principally owed his greatness, when he found that man strongly opposed to granting him the crown matrimonial, which would have enabled him to retain his position for the term of his life even in the event of his wife's decease. With the title of King-Consort, which Mary had graciously given him, the vain youth was not content. Riccio and Darnley had been close friends prior to the marriage; but, discovering that the Italian's honesty of purpose stood in his way, the King threw himself into the hands of the Protestant lords, his former foes, with a thirst for revenge all the more fatal to himself and his victim as it was reckless and impetuous.

It has now been found that Mary did not sign the League formed at this time against the Reformed religion. What is known is that Bedford wrote to Cecil on the 14th February, 1566: "There is a League concluded between the King of Spain, the Duke of Savoy, and divers other Papist princes, for the overthrow of religion, which is come to this Queen's hands, but not yet confirmed". Mary retained her promise to her subjects, and did not join this coalition. But Darnley entered into a combination of another sort, of which the purpose was to murder his wife's secretary. George Douglas, a natural son of the Earl of Angus, laid the scheme before the King, who, heedless of the character of his kinsman, at once entered into it. Douglas then sought the aid of Lord Ruthven, who, knowing the rash and fickle nature of the King, refused to accede to the plot until Darnley solemnly swore to keep it secret from the Queen. This he did. Then Ruthven made a further bargain. Blasphemously identifying the interests of religion with a cold-blooded murder, he exacted "that the lords banished for the Word of God might return to their country and their estates". Darnley agreed to the condition provided that they undertook to obtain for him the object of his ambition—the crown matrimonial. Riccio had convinced the Queen of the unfitness of her husband for a position of such authority; hence Darnley's action. Riccio had advised her Majesty to carry out the forfeiture of the estates of the rebellious Moray and his accomplices; hence the action of these lords.

Her native Caledonia, stern and wild in its scenery, must have felt to Mary strangely different from those sunny plains of France, where she had spent nearly ten years of quiet, playful, cloister-like life; where she had enjoyed more than two years and a half of wedded happiness; where for sixteen months, seated on the throne beside their monarch, she had commanded the respect and admiration of all true and loyal hearts " in a nation of men of honour and of cavaliers "; where, after three centuries of change and trouble, her memory is still fresh and green in cottage and in castle, and her name enkindles the enthusiasm of the most gifted men of letters. The people of her capital were no longer the merry commons of her infancy. Hard Reformed ways had taken the place of pastime and festival, relieving the drudgery of daily toil. She had yet to learn—and shortly, in all its intensity, did learn—that " sorrow's crown of sorrow is remembering happier things ".

## Chapter IV.

### Riccio murdered: Moray suddenly re-enters Edinburgh.

> A door flew wide, I saw them there—
>   Ruthven in mail complete,
> George Douglas, Ker of Fawdonside,
>   And Riccio at their feet;
> With rapiers drawn and pistols bent,
>   They seized their wretched prey;
> They wrenched his garments from her hand,
>   And stabbed him where he lay.
> —Aytoun.

THE night of the 9th of March, 1566, has left a stain on our national character only less deep than that marked by another tragic scene which we shall have too soon to rehearse. While Mary was at supper with some of her suite, Morton, and his kinsman George Douglas, Ruthven, Lindsay, Andrew Ker, and Patrick Bellenden, followed by a crowd of armed retainers, entered Holyrood, and there these ignoble men, while Darnley pinioned the arms of the Queen, basely stabbed David Riccio, in her very presence, dragged him forth and left his body pierced with fifty wounds. John Knox declared this deed to be "a most just act, and worthy of all praise". The conspirators then tried to keep Mary, then in the sixth month of her pregnancy, a close prisoner in her own chamber, Darnley playing king in his own small way, as if all the royal authority were already transferred to him. But the Queen was more than a match for the conspirators. In the reaction of remorse her husband came again under her influence, and she induced him to escape with her by a midnight flight to Dunbar; from thence Darnley issued a proclamation shamelessly denying all complicity with an act of such open treason. This broke up the gang. Morton and Ruthven fled into England. Moray, who had for some time previously been residing at Newcastle, watching with eager expectation the course of events, returned slily and suddenly to Edinburgh on the day after, or on the very night of the murder. He came to reap the fruits of the crimes which he had encouraged others to perpetrate. The Parliament was dissolved, and his estates were saved from immediate forfeiture. The act of dissolution was treasonable, because it wanted the Queen's consent. One purpose of the conspirators had, however, been accomplished: they had saved their rebel confederates from the punishment which their treason entailed. But how were they to colour the detention of their Queen as a prisoner, or the outrage which had been perpetrated in the royal presence? Their intention in this respect is clear beyond question. They had made up their minds to represent Riccio as her paramour, and to wrench the crown from her head on the charge of adultery, a charge, which, if available, would have emptied in that age perhaps every other throne in Europe. But Darnley, a mere tool for the moment in the hands of the conspirators, speedily gave the lie to this foul invention, and his flight with his wife showed incontestably his conviction of her innocence.

Riccio was assailed by the Queen's side, his murder was accomplished almost in her own apartment, within three months of her delivery. On the 19th of June, 1566, the future James the Sixth of Scotland and the First of England was born. His birth preceded his father's death just seven months, and occurred within three months of the poor Italian's assassination.

"THE GOOD EARL OF MORAY" had showed his gratitude to the sister who had conferred upon him one of the highest titles in her kingdom, and enriched him with many broad lands on which he had no more claim than any other bastard, by being the first to sign the document which sealed the fate of her secretary. He is known to have now used his influence to get the murderers sheltered in England, and in a letter to his sister he condemns in very strong language the men who perpetrated "the late atrocious murder". Mary, forgiving beyond all measure, took this brother, doubly base, again into favour. She pardoned the cruelties he led her into during her Northern progress, pardoned his selfish opposition to her marriage, pardoned his rebellion, pardoned his intercourse with her enemies in England, pardoned his complicity in the slaughter of her servant. Such weakness in a sovereign cannot be justified. No wonder if every high-placed ruffian in the kingdom saw that he could dare with impunity any crime, however ruthless in itself, however loathsome to men of honesty and honour. To Moray and his faction Darnley became soon after an object of vindictive abhorrence as well as contempt — Moray forgetting that, after all, the wayward and misguided young man was the husband of his benefactress, and not so guilty as himself.

## Chapter V.

### King Henry threatening to go abroad.

> Grant, O Lord, whate'er of me proceed,
> Be to Thy glory, honour, and praise indeed.
> —*Mary's prayer at the birth of her son.*

AFTER the Prince's birth, the Queen and Darnley lived happily for a short season; but before autumn Darnley's vile conduct and habitual drinking evidently distressed the poor Queen so much that Moray and Maitland took advantage of her chagrin to press upon her the advisability of a divorce. The Queen stoutly resisted a proposal for which there was no adequate cause. The King was young and thoughtless. Time might alter his ways. In any case she chose to suffer in silence rather than entertain the thought of putting asunder that which God had joined.

At this date (August, 1566), the Earl of Lennox wrote the Queen, informing her that his son, her husband, meant to go abroad. In spite of the coarseness of Darnley, Mary's conduct showed that she still loved the heartless lad, and she tried to win him back to common decency of action. At her bidding he condescended to return to Holyrood, where she received him with all the old tenderness, and reasoned with him on the wrong he was about to do himself and her by leaving the country.

Mary is said to have pleaded with him against this resolve for a whole night without success. She assembled her Council, sent for the French Ambassador next morning, and entreated Darnley in their presence to say how she had offended him. In a letter, still extant, of date 15th October, 1566, we are told that Mary took her husband by the hand, "and entreated him for God's sake to declare if she had given him any occasion for this resolution (to leave her and the country), and entreated he might deal plainly and not spare her". Darnley declared before the Council that he had no grounds at all for complaint against the Queen. Yet he left, saying, "Adieu, madam; you shall not see my face for a long time". The French Ambassador, from whose letter I have quoted, adds: "There is not one person in all this kingdom, from the highest to the lowest, that regards him any further than is agreeable to the Queen; and I never saw her Majesty so much beloved, esteemed, and honoured, nor so great a harmony amongst all her subjects, as at present is, by her wise conduct".

The Privy Council's record of this matter contains the following significant passages: "The King had no ground of complaint, but, on the contrary, had reason to look on himself as one of the most fortunate princes in all Christendom, could he but know his own happiness. They who perpetrated the murder of the Queen's faithful secretary got into her chamber with the King's knowledge. They followed at his back, and they named him chief of their enterprise. Yet the Queen never accused him thereof, but did always excuse him, and willed to appear as if she believed it not against the King; and so far was she from ministering to him occasion of discontent, that, on the contrary, he had all the reason in the world to thank God for giving him so wise and virtuous a person as she had showed herself to be in all her actions." The same record states that Darnley refused to enter the palace in consequence of the presence there of three of his co-conspirators — Mr. Froude says they were Lethington, Moray, and Argyle—but his forgiving wife condescended to meet him outside the palace, and conducted him into her own apartment, where he remained all night.

The question may be here asked—Why did Darnley make that threat to leave the country? The plain and obvious answer is that he knew that Mary loved him, and he was base enough to try to use that influence in gaining for himself the coveted crown matrimonial. If Mary had wished to be rid of him, as her enemies affirm, how could his threat to leave her have given her pain? Had she disliked him, she would have been but too glad to let him go. But, as Mr. Caird says, "the mean game which Darnley played, at his father's suggestion, was to put a strain on her affections to force her into compliance". Yet, when the Queen was counselled into letting Darnley have his way, what happened? He made ostentatious preparations, he hired ships, but he never put his foot on board. Darnley, however, had beyond doubt another reason for meditating a journey to some safer country. He had plotted with traitors against his sovereign, and had betrayed them. He had been long enough in Scotland to know that from that moment his doom was sealed. The crown matrimonial might have hastened his fate; it might also have given him a chance of warding it off for a time. But neither he nor his father could have been ignorant that, if he remained in Scotland, the vengeance of his enemies would sooner or later be wreaked in his blood. A Scottish feud in the sixteenth century was as full of peril as a vendetta in Corsica or the Abruzzi.

In December preparations were made for the celebration of the baptism of the Prince. Queen Elizabeth, making a virtue of necessity, evinced an affectionate interest in the christening, and sent the Earl of Bedford to represent her. He carried with him, as a gift from the Queen of England, a massive and elaborately wrought font of pure gold. The Countess of Argyle represented Elizabeth as godmother; the ambassadors of France and of Savoy were proxies for their sovereigns as godfathers. At Stirling, on the 17th December, the holy office was performed by the Archbishop of St. Andrews, with much pomp; and in the afternoon the infant James was proclaimed Prince of Scotland, Duke of Rothesay, Earl of Carrick, Lord of the Isles, and Baron of Renfrew.

The King was absent from the ceremony, and his absence is as ill to explain as is his petulantly refusing to go with the Queen and " hold courts of justice in person throughout the realm, and especially on the Borders ".

When, indeed, the time came in the preceding October to start for the South, Darnley had refused to accompany her Majesty. " The

Border Courts were intended to be a great State progress to crush the disorders of those districts. Every man who was fit to bear arms in the adjoining counties had been summoned to meet the King and Queen at Jedburgh." Darnley's absence is said to have grieved the Queen greatly, and with reason: it was a public affront. The members of the Privy Council were with her. Lords, barons, freeholders, landed men, gentlemen, and substantial yeomen from Edinburgh, Haddington, Berwick, Selkirk, Peebles, Lanark, Linlithgow, Stirling, Clackmannan, Kinross, were there; but the King was not in his place, and no excuse could be discovered for his absence. Another mischance came to throw into confusion the important business which had called her Majesty to the Border. The Earl of Bothwell, Lord-Lieutenant of the Marches, was lying at his Castle of Hermitage, suffering from dangerous wounds received in an encounter with Eliot of the Park. It was a matter of no light consequence this absence of the Lieutenant of the Marches, chief representative of the royal authority along all the Borders. He alone could advise what was best to be done. He had in his keeping the papers without which no decision could be taken, no case tried, no judgment rendered.

Mr. Caird says: " Mary's spirits rose with the occasion. She took horse, and, accompanied by Moray, Lethington, and other members of her Council, galloped across the country to consult with Bothwell." Without seeing the Lieutenant of the Marches, the purpose of Mary's progress along the frontier of her realm was unaccomplished. Going, as her ancestors had done for centuries, to administer justice and to establish quiet on her Borders, the Queen of Scotland was bound to see her Lord Lieutenant, just as every other sovereign was in similar circumstances.

## Chapter VI.

### The Lieutenant of the Marches cannot keep the Assize.

> Hope, there was none in store for me
> Till Darnley filled his grave.
> —Aytoun.

MARY'S progress to the Border counties and the visit which she made to the Lieutenant of the Marches were considered as hurtful to her reputation in those days, when people read certain histories of Scotland not to weigh and consider, but to believe. Buchanan is credited with this passage: "The Queen flung away in haste like ane mad woman be great journeys in post in the schairp tyme of winter frost to Melrose, and then to Jedburgh," where, hearing of Bothwell's condition, "she betuke herself to her journey with ane company, as na man of honest degree would have adventured his life and his gudes amang". Authentic documents refute the tale of this venal slanderer.

The journey of the Queen of Scots to the South simply formed part of the arrangements for conducting the business of the country which had been drawn up in the month of July. The assize at Jedburgh was first appointed for the 13th of August, and then postponed until the 8th of October. Mary reached that town on the 7th, and, instead of flinging away in haste like "ane mad woman," remained there for many days, giving her whole attention to the transaction of business. She heard of the wounds which the Lieutenant had received, on the 8th; it was only on the 16th that she found herself obliged to have recourse to his assistance in the decisions she had to take on the cases that had come before her, and in the measures which had to be concerted for the future quiet of these troublesome districts. The Queen's conference with the Earl of Bothwell lasted but two hours. If evil-minded people put an evil interpretation on the rapidity with which Mary traversed the twenty miles between Jedburgh and the Hermitage, just men will remark that she travelled the same ground with the same speed back to the seat of assize, and at once resumed her work. The sharp frost must have quickened the speed and roused the mettle of her horses. It is curious and instructive to find Buchanan reviling the company in which the Queen rode across the country to the Hermitage. Moray was there, so was Lethington, so were the Lords of the Council. Moreover, Moray's wife was present and the wives of some other members of the Council. When Moray drew from the pen of Buchanan this infamous libel on his sister and sovereign, he must surely have winced to learn that he and his wife were part of "ane company as na man of honest degree would have adventured his life and his gudes amang". But let us never forget that among the list of those who "are entertayned in Scotland by pensions out of England" stands the name of "Buckannon". And the highest of authorities warns us that iniquity gives the lie to itself.

This being one of the first open charges of a feeling too tender on Mary's part for that rough Border lord, let us look at the two as best we can. The Queen is described as being "the loveliest woman in Scotland"—tall, graceful in her gait, more graceful in the dance; a fearless and active rider, competent in music and embroidery, skilful in writing. Bothwell was an ungainly moss-trooper of uncertain age. Mary was learned and scholarly: he was ignorant and coarse. She had led a blameless life: he a most foul and depraved one. From the time when she was able to form a judgment on those about her, Mary Stuart must have known what manner of man James Hepburn was. She knew that he had quite recently formed an alliance which seemed permanent with Jean Gordon, whose family was inferior to none in the kingdom, and might be trusted to avenge any wrong to their name; and yet strange rumours were afloat of coarse connections he had fallen into in other countries. Is it possible, then, to think—I do not say believe—that such a woman could have formed a violent and unlawful affection for such a man? We shall see, in the course of this condensed narrative, that the accusation is an unmitigated calumny. At this date Darnley is still alive—foolish, vain, sensual; false to his faith, to his wife, to his friends; despised by all who knew him; but that gracious woman, his wife and Queen, is true to her duty, come what may, no matter what she may have to endure.

"The occasion of the Queen's sickness is causit by thoucht and displeasure; and, I trow, from hir awin declaration to me, that the root of it is the King." This is how Lethington accounts for the illness which, at Jedburgh, immediately after her return from the Hermitage, nearly ended the career of Mary Stuart: for several hours she lay as if dead. The Secretary wrote to the Archbishop of Glasgow on the 24th October, 1566, and in that letter, in reference to the Queen's illness, said that "hir owne declaration to me was that the wite of it is the King". Some aver that she was poisoned, and owed her life solely to the strength of her constitution.

The Bishop of Ross, in another letter written about the same date, says that Mary, believing she was dying, sent for her Ministers, and among other matters implored them to be at peace with one another, urging also the need there was for more tolerant treatment of each other in religion; for, said our wise and thoughtful Mary, "It is a sair thing to ha'e the conscience pressed in sic a matter". Darnley was informed of the Queen's serious illness, yet went not near her. Mary could not but be much mortified at his coldness and neglect. The French Ambassador narrates that Darnley expressed to him how eagerly he wished that Mary would send for him. The answer of the Ambassador might have made any husband reflect. "I do not doubt the Queen's goodness; but there are few women who, after what you have done, would seek you." When the crisis of the fever was abating, he came to her bedside, and she, unable to repress suddenly the pain caused by his indifference, did not ask him to remain. Next day he again turned his back upon her. We have the evidence of several authorities that Mary was then engaged in imparting her last instructions to her Ministers and Council. Her son she recommended to the care of the Queen of England, whose heir he was in the event of her own decease. In this deeply touching address no evidence of dislike to her consort, or of anger, is to be traced. Everywhere it abounds in calm, kindly thoughts for all those who had a claim upon her remembrance. It recalls the tender-hearted dispositions of the will which she drew up when her approaching accouchement filled her with apprehensions, which were not unreasonable, after the brutal treatment she had received from her nobles during her pregnancy. Twenty-five separate bequests were then made to her husband, and opposite one cherished object she wrote: "This is the ring with which I was betrothed. I leave it to the King, who gave it to me." Do these things read as if Mary was thinking how best she could rid herself of the man who, placing on her finger that expressive symbol, had sworn to her unalterable fidelity? Yet, within six weeks—namely, on the 11th December— when Mary had recovered and was living with Darnley at Craigmillar, Moray, Lethington, Bothwell, Huntly, and Argyle combined to urge her to a divorce. Witnesses as they had been to her emotions of wifely affection, and to her high sense of duty, how dared these men obtrude such advice?

Meanwhile, the conduct of the capricious King becomes so reprehensible that he is shunned of all men. Incapable of inspiring respect, there was little about him that could make men dread his resentment. Doubtless he returned intensely enough hate for hate, but the energy of revenge was now, in his case, enfeebled by the effeminacy of vicious habits. He had lost the power and the will to oppose intrigue to intrigue and to weave plot against plot. The contempt into which he had brought himself was so great that the French Ambassador signified to him by letter that there were two entrances to the apartments of the Embassy, and should his Majesty come to secure an interview by one passage, he would leave by the other. Moreover, the Queen had committed one of those terrible blunders of policy to which her feelings of royal clemency and a certain want of foresight and sagacity rendered her so liable. Solicited by Moray, Athole, Lethington, and Bothwell, conjured by Bedford the English, and Ducroc the French Ambassador, she had pardoned the banished lords on occasion of the solemn baptism of her infant. Unwilling to disoblige both France and England, her goodness of heart made her forget her experience and got the better of her judgment. Morton, Archibald Douglas, Lindsay, and three score other banished conspirators were now free of Scotland, free to scheme as before. Darnley, whose conscience smote him, became alarmed and went to Glasgow, where his father, the Earl of Lennox, resided. There, instead of mending his ways and thus securing himself from attack, he recklessly persisted in leading a flagitious life. Had Mary found an Albert in Henry Stuart, the pages of Scotland's history would be free from many a stain, and the annals of Great Britain would command more respect from the public opinion of Europe.

At Glasgow, the King grew unwell in the early days of January, 1567, his illness shaping itself into an attack of smallpox, all the more dangerous by reason of his disorderly habits. With the knowledge of all his wrong-doing to her and to her country, did Mary at this terrible crisis in her husband's life leave him uncared for save by his enemies and that loathsome disease? No; with the instincts of a wife—all the more loving because ill-used—she went, on the 24th of January, to nurse him; went, when she herself was suffering in mind and body; went, when she well knew that husband's ailment; went, when she knew he was in communication with the Pope for a purpose which, if the Pope had received his letters and treated them seriously, would have made every Gospeller in Scotland shoulder his hagbutt and sharpen his whinger; and went, too, when she knew the sleepless hate which Moray, Morton, and all the Douglases bore to their recreant co-conspirator. Mary is said to have found her husband grateful, humble, and penitent, "willing to be advised by her in all things". Her young heart warmed again to the high-born lad whose handsome presence had so filled her imagination some two years previously. She looked forward to long and happy days of mutual love and common devotion to the welfare of their people. She hoped that the follies of Henry's youth were over—never to return.

Mary nursed her husband for several days, and then, by easy stages, they came on together to Edinburgh. "It was desirit first in Glasgow that the King should have lain at Craigmillar, but because he hadna will thereof, the purpose was altered, and conclusion taken that he should lie beside the Kirk o' Field." Darnley's disease was probably then looked upon as a kind of leprosy, and as it was against the law to take such patients into the heart of the town, the Kirk o' Field was the place reserved for them, as least likely to expose the people to infection. It was then the most salubrious part of Edinburgh. The house selected for the King belonged to John Balfour, and Darnley acted without reflection on the advice of John's brother, Sir James, the parish priest of Flisk, as deep and dark a traitor as breathed in that treacherous generation. The grounds are very much those now occupied by the University of Edinburgh. Here Mary nursed Darnley day after day, sometimes remaining over night, but generally going home to her child.

This new and unexpected reconciliation of Mary and her husband roused the hatred and the fears of those who had so long and determinedly tried to widen the breach which Riccio's murder had made between the royal couple. His old companions in that crime, the confederate nobles, begin to pretend to "see nothing but that God must send Darnley a short end, or them a miserable life," and they were not men to accept the latter horn of the dilemma. "The chief differences were that they had practised themselves in high-handed murder, and Darnley had betrayed them. Apart from the Queen, Darnley was powerless." His restoration to her confidence must have roused fear as well as hate, in the hearts of men whose long-coveted grants of land were still insecure. The last of the four years during which Mary might have revoked these grants was fast running out, and Mary, influenced by Darnley, or for Darnley's sake, was almost sure to withhold the final legal sanction to her lavish and thoughtless donations. The lust of land was the besetting sin of the age, and the dread of losing their ill-gotten gear stirred up every evil passion in the sordid nature of these degenerate Scotsmen.

> The courtiers craved all,
> The Queen granted all,
> The Parliament passed all,
> The keeper sealed all.
>
> The ladies ruled all,
> Poor Darnley spoiled all,
> Crafty Ambassadors heard all,
> And the parson smoothed it all.
>
> He that was opposed set himself against all,
> The judge pardoned all,
> Therefore unless Mary speedily amend all,
> Without the great mercy of God, the
>     devil will have it all.

These old satiric touches seem to trace not inaptly the current of feeling in Scotland outside the limited and unscrupulous class which usurped the management of the affairs of the country. The faction now set itself in earnest to the task of putting out of the way for ever poor Henry Stuart. The Abbot of Holyrood, another of those half-brothers of the Queen, told Darnley that a plot was being formed to take his life. Darnley naturally laid his information before the Queen. She, with that straightforward common sense which she never lost, sent for the Abbot, who basely denied what he had said. The King gave him the lie, weapons were drawn, and it required all the Queen's influence to prevent blood being shed. That night she wrote a long letter to her husband full of the evidences of everything else than that she was tired of him. Moray says that Mary " again confrontet the King, and my Lord of Halyruid, conform to her letter wryttin the nycht befoir". That letter was written on the 7th February. In it, amongst much else that is beautiful, we find Mary saying : " I ask no other thing of God but that you may know what is in my heart, which is yours, and that He may preserve you from all evil, at least as long as I have life, which indeed I do not value, except so far as I and it are acceptable to you ".

## Chapter VII.

### Mary little dreams of the Calamity about to fall upon her.

> I was a witness on that night
>   Of all his shame and guilt:
> I saw his outrage on the Queen,
>   I saw the blood he spilt;
> And, ere the day had dawned, I swore,
>   While spurring through the sand,
> I would avenge that treachery,
>   And slay him with my hand—
> Or, in the preacher's cherished phrase,
>   Would purge him from the land.
>                       —BOTHWELL.

THE 9th of February, 1567, was a Sunday. Our ancestors at that date had not learned to call the first day of the week Sabbath. They were innocently ignorant of the Judaising views which were to be adopted by their grandchildren under the inspiration of the Covenant. So there was to be a wedding among the servants at Holyrood, and the Queen, ever gentle and full of sympathy with the joys, as well as the sorrows, of those about her person, had, days before, promised to patronise by her presence the ceremony itself and the merry-makings of the evening. In those days, too, Scotsmen rose early and tried to get over all they had to do ere daylight waned. So the Queen had assisted at the exercises of her own faith; had witnessed the marriage of Bastien and Margaret Carwood; had paid a morning call to Darnley; had dined at the Bishop of Argyle's house with the Ambassador of Savoy, who was to start homewards on the morrow— all before seven o'clock in the afternoon. Her Majesty then proposed to pass as great a part of the evening as possible with her husband; and all the lords of her Council except Bothwell and Moray accompanied her to the Kirk o' Field. The visit lasted two or three hours, and was a sort of public, and on the part of most perhaps a reluctant, testimony to the satisfaction caused by the "good understanding and union" in which the royal couple had been living for the three preceding weeks. "The Queen," says the French Ambassador, "then withdrew to attend the bridal of one of her gentlemen, according to her promise; and if she had not made that promise, it is believed she would have remained till twelve or one o'clock" with her husband, now convalescent, and showing at last some really trustworthy signs of a change in his habits. When, after the harmless rejoicings among her domestics,

Mary Stuart laid her head on her pillow, little did she reck what woe and misery were in store for her ere the dawn of another day.

But if the Queen of Scotland dreamt not of the agony which in a few hours she would have to endure, there were many near her who could have warned her and were silent. More faithless than all, her base brother James, deserting his post as first minister, skulked away this very evening from town, and was heard to say to his friends: "This night ere morning the Lord Darnley shall lose his life". As long as Scotsmen love to transmit to their children the memorials of their race, Monday, the 10th of February, 1567, will be one of the blackest dates in their annals. About three o'clock in the morning, a terrific explosion awoke the capital of Scotland. It was soon known that Kirk o' Field, where King Henry had been staying for some time, had been blown up with gunpowder. As the grey light of the morning fell upon the place, it was seen—in the language used at the time—to be " a' dang into dross " ; and among the shrubbery, some eighty yards away from the ruins, lay the body of the King in his night-dress, with no trace of fire, or smell of gunpowder, or bruise or mark of any kind. An attendant, also in his night-dress, lay dead beside the King. They had both been strangled as they attempted to escape. The King's clothes lay beside him, and a fur pelisse lay a little way off as if he had dropped it.

"The fact being communicated to the Queen," says the French Ambassador, "one can scarcely think what distress and agony it has thrown her into." "The Queen," says Lord Herries, "tooke this misfortune with great sorrow, and did sequestrat herselfe many days from companie." These testimonies are beyond question; but the Scottish Queen, moaning in her darkened chamber of dool, had no means of measuring the extent and magnitude of her calamity. She must have recalled the dreadful night which she passed at Amboise, amid the terrified Court of France; she must have recalled the tragic scene eleven months before, when the floor of her palace was reddened with the blood of her trusty servant. But neither of these appalling misfortunes could have oppressed her with such a sense of utter isolation as this foul murder of her second husband. To whom could she look for help or counsel? Who were the assassins? What were their purposes? What would be their next step? How long would her own life be spared, and that of the infant to which she had so recently given birth? These questions she could not answer. The ground was quaking beneath her feet, and she—once more a widow ere five-and-twenty years had passed over her head—knew not what to do.

We know many things at the present day which were hidden from Mary Stuart on the 10th of February, 1567. As soon as she recovered herself from the prostration caused by the evil tidings, she gave orders to search out the assassins and to bring them to justice. But her orders were evaded, trifled with, mocked at. Of those who sat in council around her, not one but was cognisant, or aider or abettor of the atrocious plot which deprived her of her consort. The Earl of Huntly was Chancellor, and Argyle was Lord Justice-general. We know from themselves that both these earls were acquainted with the designs of the murderers, and lifted not a finger. Morton, by his own confession, was equally guilty. Lord Robert had, indeed, divulged the secret, but had twice denied his own words. Moray, fully aware of all that was to happen, had gone off, on the pretext that his wife was unwell, to revolve how best he might shape events to his own advantage. The man who can think without compassion of Mary Stuart in desolation and in tears on this 10th of February has lost the power to sympathise with human sorrow. A great deal of blame has been cast on the young and friendless

Queen for want of energy in the prosecution of the criminals. But those who blame forget to inquire who was sheriff of the county, who were the magistrates of Edinburgh, who was Lord Justice-general, who acted as her Prime Minister? Surely, in the name of common sense, the responsibility for all that happened must fall upon these officials and their subordinates.

On the 11th of February, the day following, a Privy Council was held. Pity it is that the art of photography was unknown in those times. We should like to study, by its help, the features of the men who sat in that meeting. The proceedings were perhaps the most shameless farce that can be discovered in the records of justice. A reward of £2000 and a grant of land was offered to any who should discover the King's murderer.

Two women who lived in the neighbourhood of the Kirk o' Field were examined as witnesses, and they deponed that the noise of the explosion caused them to look into the street, and they counted nineteen men running in the direction of the city. When asked, one of the two said that she was in " hir bed wi' hir twins when she heard the crack. She ran to the door in hir sark, and she heard her neighbour Barbara Martin flytin' wi' the men who were running past, and calling them traitors." The other woman, Meg Crocket, said that she took hold of one of the men as he passed her door; that his cloak was of silk; that he shook her off; that there was armour underneath the cloak; and the man, after shaking her off, ran on without speaking. She also heard some one cry, "Oh, mercy, my cousins". The Douglases were Darnley's cousins. A large number of the actual perpetrators of this crime were from the first suspected, and they were not long in dragging in the Queen's name as some shelter to themselves. And it cannot be doubted that the original contrivers of the plot enticed others to join them by bribes and threats, alleging the Queen's sanction or connivance—a device all the more plausible as they held the highest positions in her Council.

Such and such-like were the measures taken by the Supreme Council of the realm of Scotland for tracing out the murderers of their King! Instead of taking the evidence of Meg Crocket, why did they not send for the Earl of Moray and put him to the question? And the woman who heard Barbara Martin "flytin' wi' the men," was she likely to throw more light on the mystery than the Earl of Morton.

While the Council was engaged in deliberations tending beyond doubt to deceive their sovereign and screen the authors of the murder, other rumours filled the air.  We are told that Mary had a letter from her Ambassador in Paris warning her of some impending danger, and advising her to double her guards.  To use the Queen's own words, " This warning comes too late"; and if the correspondence came through England, the delay may be accounted for. The machinations of the conspirators had pervaded France ere they reached the ears of the Queen of Scotland.  " The matter," she said, in writing to the Ambassador, " is horrible, and so strange as the like has never been heard of in any country."  Men at first naturally blamed Moray and Morton, as everybody knew them to be personal enemies of the King.  And after three centuries of keen research, the natural instinct of the public has not been found at fault.  Then Melville says: " Everybody suspects Bothwell".  There were not a few who could hint how James Hepburn had been led to do the deed.  Then Catharine de Medici was charged with some dark scheme which required the removal of King Henry; then Queen Elizabeth was suspected of an intention to destroy at one blow two dreaded aspirants to the English crown.  On the morning after the King's burial, 15th February, 1567, a placard was affixed to the door of the Edinburgh Tolbooth, charging "Earl Bothwell, Sir James Balfour, David Chalmers, and Black John Spens with the murder of the King, and that the Queen was assisting thereto through the persuasion of the Earl of Bothwell and the witchcraft of the Lady Buccleuch"; but this placard did not state who was responsible for its wording and publication. A brother of David Riccio and three French servants of the royal household were also blamed by placard; voices in the night were heard to couple the names of the Queen and Bothwell.

The Queen's enemies charged Mary with being then at Dunbar with Bothwell. Drury, ever catering for Elizabeth's weakness for scandal and gossip, chronicles this malevolent report. But Mary was at Seton Castle by the stringent order of her physician, and Bothwell was with his brother-in-law, the Earl of Huntly, at Holyrood in charge of the prince; and knowing the excellency of telling a lie, with a circumstance, Drury, in language which betrays his knowledge of coming events, adds that the Countess of Bothwell "is extremely sick and not likely to live—being marvellously swollen". Well, this "swollen" lady did not die until fully sixty years after. Divorced from Bothwell, she became, in 1573, the wife of Alexander, eleventh Earl of Sutherland; and, on his death in 1594, she married Alexander Ogilvie of Boyne, dying as late as 1629. Need we wonder that, crushed in spirit, physically unnerved, oppressed by an atmosphere laden with treachery, the young Queen should turn her thoughts to that land where she had spent her early and happy years? Mary asked her relatives to allow her to go to France; but from a letter of the 15th March, 1567, from Don Francis de Alara to Philip, we find that her proposal was not welcomed: " The Queen of Scotland is anxious to come to this kingdom to live in some town assigned to her as dower, but here they are opposed to her coming, and do their utmost to induce her to remain where she is". Does this show any indication of that "infatuated love for Bothwell" which her traducers ascribe to her? He, without doubt, was aiming at the crown and the Queen—a fact of which Drury and the English government were aware before Mary Stuart; but where have we any evidence that Mary in any way encouraged his ambition? Within a month, however, after Darnley's death, the conspirators, unflagging in their fell designs, had managed to fix suspicion on Bothwell and their Queen. When her kindred of Lorraine sent Mary, young as she was, into a den of robbers and demons, as Scotland then was; when they abandoned her to her fate; when they refused to allow her to return to France, they committed, for reasons of French State policy, one of the grossest cruelties in history.

Henry Stuart was young, and age might have corrected his ways, but as the facts stand he had proved a bad husband; to gainsay this, one would require the effrontery of Buchanan, more than the stubborn courage of Mr. Froude. In these circumstances it might have been possible for Mary to obtain relief by a judicial separation from bed and board. Far from desiring this, Mary would not give her consent to his leaving the country even for a short season. She was pained when he was not by her side during her progress on the Borders. His absence rendered her illness at Jedburgh all the more dangerous to her life, and one day's short visit during her convalescence was a consolation which deepened her distress at his rude departure on the morrow. His preference for the society of his father, and of his kinsmen in the western shires, always grieved her, and was in all probability intended to cause her vexation. His shameless infidelities, coarse talk, and low associations were to her a constant source of misery. Yet what is the language in which

Mary puts aside the request of her "chief nobility" to sanction some device to free her of Darnley's presence? "I will that ye do nothing whereby any spot may be laid upon my honour or my conscience. Therefore, I pray you, rather let the matter be in the state that it is, abiding till God of His goodness put remedy thereto." This is unmistakably the language of a pure woman and a faithful wife. They had been married only eighteen months and eleven days; Mary hoped to the last for better things of the man to whom she had given her heart; and who can blame her?

Mary's first husband died blessing her for her goodness. Is there anything to show that a second marriage, necessary to assure the peace of her dominions by providing indisputable succession to the crown, had turned a gentle, warm-hearted woman into a lustful fiend? Facts prove the contrary: if she had much to suffer, her heart did but pour forth its treasure of affection in proportion as it was crushed. When Mary went to Glasgow and nursed her husband through a loathsome and deeply contagious ailment, was this exposure of her life and person a mere sham? Pretending to forgive, did she lavish all her tenderness on him only that she might entice him from Glasgow and his father's care to hand him over to those who had sworn, with her knowledge, to kill him?

Basely wronged by her subjects, Mary Stuart had a neighbour and cousin, who, by every artifice in her power, was ever trying for English interests to stir up mischief. There is more than a suspicion that Elizabeth was privy to the plot for Darnley's destruction. One important letter remains of all those which are known, like Darnley's papers, to have been destroyed. In it Drury, writing to Cecil, says: "The King was long of dying, and to his strength made debate for his life. It was Captain Cullen's persuasion for more surety to have the King strangled, and not to trust to the train of powder alone, affirming that he had known many so saved. Sir Andrew Ker, with others, was on horseback near unto the place for aid, if need had been." Andrew Ker, so placed, is the same as he who, on the night of Riccio's murder, pointed his pistol at Mary's breast. This miscreant had been specially exempted from the pardon which enabled Morton and the others to return. He was still an outlaw, and must have passed the Border with the permission or connivance of the English Wardens.

Was it likely that this villain would have come to render service to Mary? Would the Queen of Scotland have taken the help of one stained with the crime which had deprived her of one of her most capable assistants in carrying on the business of her government? If this Andrew Ker was not in the employment of Moray, or of the English Ministry, what was his purpose? Those who despatched him on his errand must have known not only the time but also the place of the intended assassination.

It is strange that a certain class of writers who assume that Mary Stuart had conceived a guilty passion for James Hepburn, and then proceed to argue that she was an accomplice in King Henry's murder, deal so differently with the case of Elizabeth. The liberties which, in the presence of the Scottish Ambassador, Elizabeth allowed herself with her favourite are very significant. The bitterest enemy of Mary Stuart has never discovered such doings at the Court of Holyrood. Elizabeth's passion for Leicester is a matter of doubt only to those who, in spite of accumulating evidence, hug the legend of the Virgin Queen in growing despair. That Amy Robsart was done to death is an indisputed fact. Mary had seen and known and disliked Bothwell from her earliest years. The graceful and handsome courtier whom she made Earl of Leicester was not looked at with indifference by the daughter of Henry the Eighth. The uncouth Lieutenant of the Marches had little to recommend him besides his courage and his loyalty to his country. He was ugly, witless, mannerless. He led a most loose life. He professed attachment to the new faith. When he married Jean Gordon, "the Queen wished the nuptials to be solemnised in the Palace Chapel according to the old rites. But no entreaties could overcome Bothwell's tender regard for the Protestant religion: the conscience which smiled at murder and adultery was appalled by the forms of a heterodox belief, and the marriage vows, which he was to break almost as soon as they were made, were blessed by a Protestant preacher in the face of a Protestant congregation." Is it at all possible to believe that Mary, brought up as she was by a relative whose virtues were the admiration of all France, could have even cared for this man, still less nursed a licentious passion for him, as her enemies assert? We contend that Bothwell's personal appearance, his uncultured mind, his evil reputation, and his Protestantism are reasons why Mary would never have thought of him for a husband. Had she desired to make James Hepburn her paramour, there would have been no necessity for murdering anybody. The Courts of England and the Continent presented many examples of illicit love, which she had but to follow. Faunt says that he never saw "so little godliness" and "so dissolute manners" as in the Court of Elizabeth. "All enormities reigned there." "There was no love there," adds Harrington, "but that of the lusty god of gallantry Asmodeus." Why did John Knox roar against Mary and blow soft on Elizabeth?

The Earl of Lennox had not appeared at Court since Riccio's murder. Instead of hastening to her side when she announced the assassination of his son, this cold-hearted father-in-law commenced a correspondence with the bereaved Queen about ten days after. In one of his letters, dated from his Castle of Houston, in Renfrewshire, 20th February, 15 7, he thanks the Queen for her "most gracious and comfortable letter, and suggests that, as the delinquents are not discovered, Parliament should be summoned to devise the best means of accomplishing that object". Why did he not apply to Argyle?

Mary's immediate reply was a letter from Seton Castle, of next day's date, telling him that before the receipt of his yesterday's letter she had summoned "Parliament, in which first of all this matter (being most dear to her) shall be handled, and nothing left undone which may further the clear trial of the same". Lennox, in his next letter, seeing that the Queen had anticipated his suggestion by having already called Parliament together, says: "The time is long to Parliament," and that "The matter in hand is not a Parliament matter, but ought rather to be with all diligence sought out and punished". It may be true that a Scottish Parliament was never called upon to discharge the functions of a county sheriff, or of a modern procurator-fiscal. But, if so, why did the Earl of Lennox not apply to Argyle, who was Lord Justice-general?—why not to Huntly, the Chancellor? —why not to his old comrade in treason, the Earl of Moray, who then performed in the government of Scotland the duties of Prime Minister? If Parliament could do nothing, what could the Queen do?

According to the notions prevalent among Scotsmen of the sixteenth century, it was almost a sacred duty for Lennox to avenge the assassination of his son. To have recourse to justice was praiseworthy only in so far as justice was an instrument of vengeance. But in Earl Matthew's letters we discern little of that fierce anger and relentless revenge which animated his brother nobles, and left them no peace until they had seen his son stark and stiff in the garden of the Kirk o' Field. Yet the injury which they had suffered at the hands of

King Henry was slight in comparison with that which they had inflicted upon King Henry's father. Lennox proceeds to say that he has heard the names of certain persons mentioned as being guilty of the King's murder, and entreats the Queen to have such persons forthwith apprehended. The Queen asks him eagerly to give her the names. Her letter is of date 1st March; Lennox, with unaccountable remissness, delays his reply until the 17th. He gives the names already mentioned, adding, after the name of Joseph Riccio, " I assure your Majesty I for my part greatly suspect this man". Was this because his son's dagger was found sticking in the body of " this man's " brother? The Queen summoned a Council of her nobles for the end of March, and urged Lennox to attend. Lennox did not think proper to attend; but an order was made on the 28th March for the trial of Bothwell. At his trial the Earl of Lennox did not appear, but wrote from Stirling saying he was sick, and requesting that the trial meanwhile should be stayed, " that he might have sufficient time to seek for manifestations of this most odious crime"; and he requested the Queen to grant him her commission for apprehending such persons as he should be informed were present at the murder of his son. This was a demand which the members of Mary's Privy Council were not likely to listen to; nor can we see what would have resulted from the apprehension of Joseph Riccio. Earl Matthew's conduct appears to be one-half that of a dupe, the other half that of an accomplice.

The accusers of Mary Stuart assert that the trial, which at his repeated instance was granted to the Earl of Bothwell, was a collusive one. And judging by the light which discussion has thrown on the proceedings, we do not hesitate to assert that it was so. But the collusion was not contrived by the Queen, but by the faction of assassins who filled her council-chamber, who, along with the prisoner in the dock, had planned the crime, worked out the details of its execution, and had given written bonds to safeguard its perpetrators from punishment. When we know that Maitland and Morton rode by Bothwell's side to the Tolbooth, that Argyle presided as Justice-general, that Lord Lindsay, one of Riccio's murderers, and James MacGill, and Henry Balnaves—all old offenders—supported Argyle on the bench, the inference is unavoidable. These men were sworn to see their tool and confederate scathless, and their selfish interests required that they should not break their oaths. On the 9th of April, three days before the trial, Moray, fearing the necessity of showing his colours, stole out of the country. Pretending to pass over to France, he went to England, and there propagated malignant insinuations against his royal sister. The discoveries of recent years inform us that this heartless hypocrite, just six days before his departure, executed a will for which there was little urgency, bequeathing his child to the care of the sister whom he was undermining and defaming. There is this much to be said for James Hepburn, that he persistently insisted upon being put on his trial, while all the other nobles accused by the public voice avoided such a risk. He was not a hypocrite, he audaciously brazened out his crimes and their consequences.

Two days after the trial, Parliament assembled. Instead of appearing in his place, the Earl of Lennox, who had so repeatedly sought such an occasion of avenging the death of his son, followed Moray to England on the 17th April. I do not believe that Earl Matthew was so much afraid of Bothwell as has been said. His real enemy was Argyle, who had availed himself of every opportunity to plunder the possessions of the house of Lennox in the west, and was determined, now that Darnley was out of the way, to keep what he had taken. And in such a cause the confederates might be trusted to stand by Mac-Callum-Mohr. Indeed without giving special attention to the proceedings of this Parliament, no one can hope to thread his way through the intrigues, the crimes, and the ever varying combinations of this repulsive period of Scottish history. In proportion as our knowledge of it increases, the stronger becomes our conviction that in the minds of the Scottish nobles in the sixteenth century self-interest preceded every other consideration. Mary Stuart had an inordinate belief in human gratitude, and when solicited seldom refused. The lands attached to the monasteries, the churches, and the hospitals had failed to satisfy the rapacity of her ministers and their adherents. Two-thirds of the property of the Crown disappeared amongst them. Yet, as Chalmers justly observes, the confirmation of all these lands at this time to such profligate characters as Moray and Morton only induced them to attack their too generous Queen with greater boldness.

First and foremost in the harvest of iniquity comes the Earl of Moray, Prior of St. Andrews, of Pittenweem, and of Maçon in France. This "stickit priest" blossoms forth in the records of this Parliament into one of the most powerful lords in the kingdom. Of the twenty-four Acts passed, that which confirms his titles and estates is the greatest and most elaborately framed. As now printed it occupies eight columns of the largest folio. And while these confirmations were being ratified, what was James Stuart doing? He was slandering and working the ruin of his royal sister at the Court of England, and hastening to do the same at the Court of France. Next appears James Douglas, Earl of Morton, who, over and above the confirmation of his titles and acquisitions, received for his nephew, a boy twelve years old, the great Earldom of Angus with its vast domains, which belonged by right to Lord Darnley, and through him to the royal infant then in his cradle at Stirling. And of course the Maitlands came in for a large share of the spoils. Huntly, Bothwell, Rothes, follow in due order with many others whom it were tedious to enumerate. Who did the deed? asks the ancient Roman law in every criminal investigation. The answer guides us like a pillar of light through the deceiving politics of this darkened period of our annals. "They did it who profited by it."

One Act, however, and a very significant one, was passed, for which Mary never, during the next hundred years, got the credit she deserved. She was at the time charged with attempting to suppress the reformed religion. Yet this Act renounced all foreign jurisdiction in ecclesiastical affairs, and gave toleration to all to worship God in their own way!

Bothwell was assiduous in his attendance on this Parliament, and his friends, Maitland and Morton, secured for him a very remarkable document, signed by several lords of Moray's faction and eight bishops, in which they own their belief in the innocence of Bothwell of the charge of murdering the King, and, though handfasted to another woman, they name him as fittest husband for the Queen. It is said that on that memorable night at Ainslie's Tavern the nobles drew cuts as to which of their number was to become third husband to the Queen. The winning cut was drawn by Bothwell. In some degree to cover this atrocious arrangement, the tricky Maitland prepared a forged consent by the Queen to a marriage with Bothwell. The plain English of all this intriguing is, that the scheming villains were to keep what they had got and to look for more; the Crown was to be despoiled, and the lady who wore it was to be made the victim of one man's mad lust and ambition, and the sport of them all.

The course of our narrative thus brings us

to perceive how these noble criminals, like the vilest thieves and murderers in our police reports, were led on from one crime to another. They had slain King Henry, as their ancestors were believed to have slain fifty-six of his predecessors. They were gorged with the spoils of the Church and the Crown. But they were not at ease or content. As far as they could, they had taken from their sovereign the power of revoking what she had granted with youthful generosity. But ill-defined as the Scottish constitution was, Queen Mary possessed by uncontested and immemorial precedent the power to recall all these donations until she had completed her twenty-fifth year, and she had yet nearly eight months to exercise that constitutional prerogative. Their alarm was increased by another circumstance. Mary was allied to the noblest houses in Europe, and was still in the fresh bloom of early womanhood. Suitors from the Continent were sure to seek her hand, and her choice might fall on one who possessed the power and the ability to curb rebellion in her dominions, and to check treasonable intercourse with her neighbours on the southern side of the Tweed. If they were to proceed as they had begun, there were but two courses open to them: they must either find means to bring her "a short end," or they must constrain her to marry some one on whom they could place some reliance. Afraid of incurring universal execration if they imbrued their hands in the blood of a Queen, they adopted the latter course. Their deliberations resulted in the infamous meeting called "Ainslie's supper," and we shall now see how their project sped.

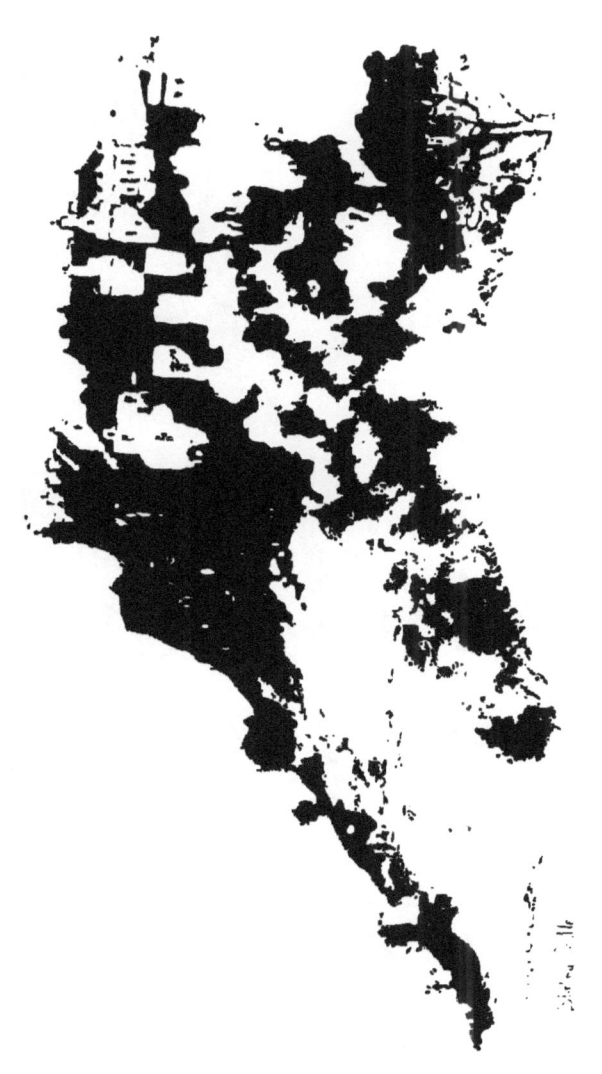

## Chapter VIII.

### Mary trembles for the Safety of her Child.

> Bothwell, that despotic man, ruled thee with shameful, overbearing will, and with his philtres and his hellish arts. . . . No! no! all the arts he used were man's superior strength.
> —Schiller.

THE atrocity of the Kirk o' Field made the Queen of Scots tremble for the safety of her child. She resolved, therefore, to entrust the care of the boy, around whom her affections and hopes now clung all the closer, to John Erskine, Earl of Mar, who had watched with fidelity over the early years of her own childhood. Mar was governor of Stirling Castle, and on the 19th of March, Huntly and Argyle carried the infant prince within the strong walls of that ancient fortress. Thus at the date which we have now reached the royal widow had not seen her child for a whole month. In any circumstances a youthful mother so long separated from her first-born would feel uneasy and anxious. In Mary Stuart's case this pain was increased by recent sufferings of the deepest kind, and by many apprehensions of evil. Seizing the first opportunity, she started on Monday, the 21st of April, from Lord Seaton's. She could not rest until she had assured herself with her own eyes of the welfare of the babe whose feeble thread of life had been exposed to such risk ere she had ushered him into the world, and who, notwithstanding all her precautions, might be as seriously menaced at any moment. The jealousy of our nobles had never permitted our sovereigns to maintain a guard suited to their position, and Mary, our first Queen, reigning in her own right, was on this, as on other journeys, obliged to content herself with a number of attendants less than that which often followed the heels of a bonnet laird.

Birrel, Knox, and Spottiswood have found nothing more in Queen Mary's journey to Stirling than the visit of an anxious mother to her first-born child. The inventive genius of George Buchanan, however, has imagined quite another motive. George undertakes to persuade us that the Earl of Bothwell longed to have the heir to the crown in his hands; that he induced the Queen to endeavour to get her boy out of the Earl of Mar's keeping; but that the Earl, suspecting some such design, made her Majesty content herself with a distant look at his charge. Buchanan's insinuation—quite in the style of Moray, his paymaster—is too broad to be mistaken. The Queen, according to George, was planning with Bothwell how best to make away with her child. When George penned this slander, the generous woman, who, for some lessons in Latin and for some fulsome Latin verses, had given him the revenues of the rich lands of Crossraguel, had no more lands to give to anybody. With unerring instinct George was turning his hungry eyes in another direction.

I might well content myself with refuting this disgraceful insinuation in Mary's own words. "The natural love which a mother bears to her only bairn is sufficient to confound" those who repeat it; "it needs no other answer". But what motive, let me ask, could Mary Stuart have for committing so unnatural a crime? Her boy's life strengthened those claims of succession to the throne of England which she was always labouring to secure, which she was too often putting inopportunely forward. Her boy inherited those titles which in marrying Henry Stuart she had joined to her own. The destruction of the infant James would inevitably have raised up for her a competitor in the person of Lord Charles, Darnley's brother. In point of fact, she knew that King Henry's body was scarcely laid in the grave ere the Earl of Lennox was already talking of the presumptive rights of his second son.

Emulous of Buchanan's audacity, Mr. Froude considers that people in the nineteenth century are soft enough to believe the following story which he has given himself the trouble to re-edit from Drury's correspondence. "The Prince being brought to" the Queen at Stirling, "she offered to kiss him, but the Prince would not, but put her face away with his hand, and did to his strength scratch her. She took an apple out of her pocket and offered it, but it would not be received by him. The nurse took it, and to a greyhound bitch having whelps she threw the apple. The bitch ate it, and she and her whelps died presently. A sugar loaf also for the Prince was brought thither at the same time and left for the Prince, but the Earl of Mar keeps the same. It is judged to be very evil compounded."

It is good for honest people that calumnious scribes like Buchanan and Drury are usually at variance. According to the former, the Queen was only permitted to look at her boy. According to the latter, she was allowed to offer to kiss the Prince; and the child being in a fractious humour, was certainly not hindered from doing his very best to scratch her Majesty.

No natural history that we are acquainted with attributes to dogs any special liking for apples. It is true that pets may be schooled into marvellous things in the way of eating, yet in the sixteenth century greyhounds were generally trained by hard kinds of food for stiff coursing over the heather and in the stubble fields. The bitch that ate Drury's apple may be pardoned for dying so quickly, but as the whelps are not said to have had any share of the fruit, it is difficult to excuse them for dying at the same precise moment. Did Drury, does Mr. Froude, mean to assure us that apples were ripe on the northern side of the Tweed on the 22nd of April, 1567? If so, it is to be deplored that the climate of the "land o' cakes" has so woefully changed.

Mr. Froude had better make a short trip next April to France, where Mary spent the happy days of her youth. He will there find the shop windows gay with fruit and fish of many kinds made of sugar, and on inquiry he will be told what place the "poissons d'avril" have long held in the manners and customs of our Gallic neighbours. Drury's childish tale has simply this foundation, that Mary Stuart had seen April fish and fruit presented in France to children of all ages, and thought that something of the same kind would be a nice little treat to her own little boy on her first visit to him in the month of April. Drury was certainly one of those envoys who were sent to lie abroad for Elizabeth's behoof and delectation, but I doubt whether he gave this silly gossip for gospel. As Mr. Froude does not recognise the necessity of examination before committing himself to a statement, he has himself to blame if the public set him down as a writer who systematically travesties and omits facts for artistic and argumentative purposes.

The chequered life of the Queen of Scotland has furnished abundant matter to poets and writers of tragedy and romance. And certainly no events can be more startling than those which it is now our task to record. On the morning of the 23rd of April, the Queen left Stirling, slept in the place of her birth, Linlithgow Palace, and the following day continued her journey to the capital. Yet distant from the city some six or seven miles, she was met by the Earl of Bothwell, who was Sheriff of the county of Edinburgh, at the head of 800 spearmen, whom he had assembled under pretext of an expedition against the freebooters of Liddesdale. The place was called Foulbriggs, surely a most appropriate name, and lies between two bridges, one crossing the Almond, the other the Gogar Burn. As Mr. Chalmers observes, "it is of all places on the road from Linlithgow to Edinburgh that which Bothwell might be expected to choose". Certainly none seems to afford greater facilities for attacking and overpowering a small party on its way eastwards. So large a force of spearmen, commanded by the chief magistrate of the shire on which she had just entered, must have filled the Queen with alarm and dread. The Earl assured her that she was exposed to new and greater dangers, and that in accordance with his duty he had hastened to protect her.

But the Queen's agitation was not calmed by this plausible explanation, and it is not easy to discover what Huntly the Chancellor, and Maitland the Secretary, and Sir James Melville, who were in attendance upon her Majesty, did or said to throw light on Bothwell's proceedings. Rumours of new plots and combinations had been in the air, and it is now certain that these three men could have given the Queen more information than they did. Bothwell implored her Majesty to seek protection in the Castle of Dunbar, which he held in his possession as High Admiral. And, adding violence to entreaty, as the cavalcade drew near to the walls of Edinburgh, he seized the Queen's horse by the bridle, while his men laid hold of Huntly, Lethington, and Melville. Immediately the whole body of horsemen, leaving the road to the gates of the city, swept the Queen's small party with them in the direction of Dunbar. When the drawbridge of that gloomy fortress rose, Mary Stuart must have begun to see that she was the victim of an abduction as brutal and abominable as perhaps any recorded in the annals of mankind.

Queen Mary's visit to Hermitage Castle during her progress on the Borders—prescribed by duty, yet misinterpreted by factious malevolence—obliged me to draw attention to the appearance and character of James Hepburn, Earl of Bothwell. It is now necessary to complete my portraiture of this notorious personage. James Hepburn was a compound of virtues not at all common among our ancestors of the sixteenth century, and of vices to which all his contemporaries abandoned themselves without shame. No one of his rank was more loyal to his sovereign, no one was truer to Scotland. Neither English nor French gold ever polluted his hands. And as often happens in like circumstances, he whose loyalty was the more conspicuous because unique profited all the less by his services to the State. The honours or offices which he held came to him as a sort of inheritance from his father and grandfather; they were not, as prejudiced writers assert, marks of favour bestowed upon him by Mary Stuart. His grandfather had been appointed High Admiral by James IV. in 1511, and had received from that monarch the custody of those strongholds on the coast which required to be kept in a state of efficiency for the defence of the nation. Earl James, indeed, held the chief command on the Marches as Lord-Lieutenant during Mary's reign, but it was not Mary, but Mary's mother, the Queen Regent, who promoted him to that responsible and perilous position. And as far as fidelity and devotion to the country were concerned, Mary of Lorraine could not have made a better choice. James Hepburn had a wholesome distrust of the "South'ron loons"; he was never known to take his cue from London like Kirkaldy of Grange, or whine and fawn at the feet of Elizabeth like Moray.

Notwithstanding these rare and striking merits, Earl James was distinguished even in that bad age by the lowest vices. While Darnley's excesses were the follies of a vain, giddy, misguided, intemperate youth, Bothwell's sins were those of a villain hardened beyond the possibility of remorse. The Earl of Morton, who soared far above Bothwell in every form of rapacity, could not keep up with Bothwell in lust and lewdness. Daring as Earl James was on the field of battle and in tracking to their fastnesses the wildest marauders of the Borders, he was still more daring in attack and pursuit when his unclean appetites were inflamed. James Hepburn, too, came of a race in which the worst forms of this degrading vice had long been hereditary. One of his ancestors is accused of having carried off Jane Beaufort, the young widow of James I., to this very stronghold of Dunbar, where she died; another had sullied the reputation of Mary of Gueldres, the young widow of James II. His father, Earl Patrick, had divorced his wife, Janet Sinclair.

When Earl James, therefore, on the 24th of April, 1567, carried the twice-widowed Mary Stuart and her attendants "captive," as Melville plainly says, to Dunbar, he was but following the hereditary instincts of his family and satiating passions which a bad education and bad associates abroad had fostered beyond control. In his abduction of Queen Mary he was aided and abetted, if we are to believe an Act of Parliament, by his uncle the Bishop of Moray, and by three cousins, all parsons of whose ways and characters the less I say the better. How or why James Hepburn professed himself a Protestant I do not pretend to examine. It is certain that John Knox and his forbears were vassals of the great house of Bothwell, and that Bothwell listened to the Reformer's reprimands and sermons with exemplary humility and patience.

From the evening of the 24th of April, until the morning of the 6th of May—twelve terrible days of mental torture—the Queen of Scotland was held in the unclean grasp of this monster of lust. Her ladies-in-waiting were dismissed, and no woman was allowed to approach her but the sister of her ravisher. With his victim completely in his power, Bothwell now boasted that he would marry the Queen, who " would or would she not ; yea, whether she would herself or not ". Cherishing the hope that the news of the outrage would speedily bring an army of loyal subjects to her rescue, Mary resisted the importunities of her insolent captor. But the daring Earl had a weapon of which his victim knew nothing. He unfolded the infamous bond by which her nobles and trusted councillors had delivered up their Queen to the ambition and lust of one of the most depraved among them. Mary read the document with stupor and dismay; but the native courage of her race did not yet desert her—not even when days passed, and, as the great Sir Walter complains, "not a spear was lifted, not a sword drawn to save her from the power of that atrocious ruffian".

I would fain pass over in silence what followed, but historical exactness requires that facts which afford the key to a long train of events should be brought into proportionate prominence. It cannot be doubted that James Hepburn violated the person of his sovereign. Mary herself asserts it. James Melville states it in the plainest and crudest terms. Parliament declared that Bothwell used "unleisum" means in forcing the Queen to marry him. And Bothwell himself before his death avowed as much. It is, moreover, extremely probable that to accomplish his purpose the villain disordered his victim's brain by some narcotic potion; for he himself confessed that he administered to her "sweet waters". The common report of the time was that he employed magic or the black art, in which so many professed themselves proficient in that age. But while there is little doubt that the worst features of mesmeric science were known long before Mesmer was born, and that Bothwell had frequented the worst society abroad, yet the facts are sufficiently accounted for without this hypothesis. I give the result in Sir James' own words. "And then the Queen could not but marry him seeing he had ravished her, and lain with her against her will." Thus by matchless artifice and brutal force was Mary so surrounded that she had but one method of escape left open to her. Under Bothwell's thraldom and Maitland's collusion, in the fangs of her relentless brother's faction, what could she do but consent to this most odious union?

I am glad to find evidence that the nobility and burgesses of Aberdeen did, by special messenger, send a letter to the Queen putting their swords at her service, if she would but "certifie her mind by bearer hereof". The feeling in Aberdeen and throughout the Northland was strongly with the Queen. It had been intensified by the unfeeling treatment which nearly five years before, on the chief market-place of the city, her base-born brother had forced her to endure. But, great as that Castlegate grief was, Mary's life in the few intervening years had been filled with griefs. Not yet was her cup of sorrow full.

## Chapter IX.

### The Double Process of Divorce.

> No one can anticipate . . . how wide may be the discussions opened by this discovery.
> — Burton.

IN the interval between the Foullsbrigg occurrence and the tragedy at Dunbar, Bothwell had been taking steps, of which his confederates could not be ignorant, to get his recent marriage with Huntly's sister dissolved; and a spectacle which in our days would appear most singular presented itself. Lady Jean Gordon, who is said to have professed the Catholic religion, sued for divorce in Protestant Consistorial court. The Earl, who on all occasions had vaunted himself an uncompromising Protestant, instituted a process in the court of the Catholic Archbishop. Lady Jean's plea was the adultery of her husband. Bothwell alleged an impediment of consanguinity unremoved by any dispensation. Each plea was admirably adapted to the tribunal before which it was urged.

Like almost every other event in Queen Mary's short reign, this double process of divorce by the Earl and Countess of Bothwell has been converted into an instrument for ruining her Majesty's reputation. It is maintained by Mary's enemies that she had long been planning how James Hepburn might be separated from his Catholic wife, Jean Gordon, and that for this purpose she had restored the jurisdiction of the archiepiscopal court, which had been suppressed by the Act of August, 1560, which had swept away the authority of the Pope. But the real historical facts do not bear this interpretation. The Queen, indeed, had, by a writ under her sign-manual dated 23rd of December, 1566, allowed the Archbishop of St. Andrews to resume the exercise of his authority; but as she had never signified her royal assent to the Act of August, 1560, her Majesty did not, and could not, believe that the Archbishop's court had ever been really and legally suppressed. Nor can it be imagined that there then existed, or that their exists at present in the kingdom, any competent lawyer who would subscribe to that opinion. What induced Bothwell and Lady Jean to apply to both consistories was the uncertain state of the law, at a moment when everything was in a state of transition. What had previously urged the Queen to get the Archbishop's court to resume its work was the extreme disorder into which public and private business had been thrown by the discontinuance of its sittings. Many suits relating to wills and to the collation of benefices as well as to marriages were pending, and it was difficult to decide whether they were to be conducted before the old tribunals, or the new Protestant consistory, or the Court of Session.

And the detractors of Mary Stuart omit to mention that when Archbishop Hamilton went to Edinburgh, relying on the Queen's writ to inaugurate the restoration of his authority over the archdeaconry of the Lothians, he was prevented from doing so by the menacing attitude of the Protestant General Assembly, and by a portion of the burghers of the capital whom Moray and the ministers had roused to opposition. And we find Bedford writing on the 9th of January, 1567, to Cecil, that "at the suyte of my Lord of Murrey, the Quene was pleased to revoke that which she had before granted to the said Bishop". As a historical fact, therefore, it was not in a state of things purposely combined and matured by Mary that the Primate of Scotland, "ane comoun enemy to

Chryst," "the head of the venemous beast," was called upon to try the validity of a Protestant marriage by the "stoutest" Protestant in the realm. The situation was not created by the Queen; it was the result of the action of the General Assembly, which would not sacrifice its hatred of "idolatrie" to the general interests of the public, and of the intrigues of Moray, who claimed to be oppressed by similar scruples. Willingly or unwillingly, Archbishop Hamilton, yielding to Bothwell's summons or entreaty, issued his commission to Robert Crichton, Bishop of Dunkeld, William Chisholm, Bishop of Dunblane, and others, on Sunday, the 27th of April. And surely nothing can be more remarkable than that the men who but a few months before had so strenuously resisted the reopening of the archiepiscopal court were now deaf and dumb when the exercise of its jurisdiction was demanded by the foremost professor of the Evangel. Against this backsliding of their co-religionist, they neither drew the sword of Gideon nor quoted the heavy message of Jeremiah.

On the 5th of May only one judge-delegate appeared to receive the evidence produced by Bothwell's proctor. On the day following Lady Jean's agent made some formal objections to the proceedings renouncing all further defence.

And on the 7th sentence was pronounced, that, as far as canon law and Catholic usage were concerned, no Catholic marriage could have taken place between Jean Gordon and James Hepburn, because their relationship by blood was within forbidden degrees, and no dispensation had been obtained.

About fourteen or fifteen years ago, the accusers of Mary Stuart raised a triumphant cackle over a form of dispensation for Bothwell's marriage with Lady Jane, which the late Dr. John Stuart discovered in the charter-room of Dunrobin Castle. This form of dispensation, however, is evidently a ridiculous forgery. It cannot have been issued from the chancery of St. Andrews, or been drawn up by anyone connected with the administration of ecclesiastical affairs. It claims to have been granted in the seventh year of the pontificate of Pius IV. Now Pius IV. never saw the seventh year of his pontificate; his reign lasted only five years, eleven months, and three days, leaving the sixth year from his coronation incomplete by twenty-eight days.

Moreover, Pius IV. died during the night between the 8th and 9th of December, 1565; and before the date of this pretended dispensation—17th February, 1566—all Scotland knew that one Pope had gone to his account and another had taken his place. Michael Ghisleri had been elected on the 17th, and under the name of Pius V. had been crowned on the 17th January; and on the 31st of the same month the Queen of Scotland had written a letter of congratulation to his Holiness, and sent William, Bishop of Dunblane, with it to Rome. It is impossible in these circumstances that Archbishop Hamilton or his secretary or his datary could have been ignorant of such events; probably they were known to the Primate, who was Legatus-natus and Legate a Latere, before they had been communicated to the Court of Holyrood. And it is therefore morally impossible that a document such as that which Dr. Stuart disinterred at Dunrobin could have issued from the chancery of St. Andrews.

This document provides other arguments against its own authenticity, which our limits prevent us from noticing. When Moray alleged that Bothwell's marriage with Lady Jean had been dissolved, only because the dispensation which they had obtained had been abstracted, he may have heard some whisper of a document, which, however, had not been presented because it could not bear the light of day, and would not stand collation with the books of the archiepiscopal chancery or of the archdeaconry of the Lothians. The procedure, therefore, before the Primate's court followed the ordinary course of ecclesiastical law. If Bothwell and Jean Gordon were fully aware—and it is nearly impossible to imagine them ignorant—of their relationship, when on the 24th of February, 1566, they were joined in wedlock by Jean's uncle— a declared Protestant, though still taking the style of a Papist prelate—the marriage was, in a Catholic point of view, simply one of those handfastings which were still too common in Scotland, though the influence of the Church had been exerted against them for centuries. It was Jean Gordon's duty, if, as most writers assert, she was a sincere Catholic, first to procure a dispensation and then to celebrate her marriage in the sight of the Catholic Church, as had been required from the dawn of ecclesiastical legislation in her native country.

Was this document concocted and palmed upon her to allay any scruples she may have entertained? Did the individual who composed it count upon Lady Jean's ignorance of Latin, and of the most ordinary forms of legal deeds? Was it purposely drawn up in such terms as would make it worthless? Why was it so carefully stowed or so carelessly thrown away in the charter chest at Dunrobin? To the first couple of questions the answer is not so important. To the latter an answer suggests itself which throws a flood of light on the point I am discussing. Five years before Bothwell's death Jean Gordon entered into a contract of marriage with the Earl of Sutherland. A valid and authentic dispensation for her union with Bothwell would have prevented her from completing this new contract. On the other hand, a forged and evidently worthless dispensation proved that her union with the villainous Earl had been null and void from the beginning, and left her free from the necessity of waiting until the horrors of a Danish dungeon had done their work of retribution.

The Protestant Commissaries of Edinburgh seemed to have met with even less difficulty in their decision. James Hepburn's manner of life afforded more matter than was necessary to facilitate their deliberations. Already, on the 3rd of May, they had decided in favour of the Catholic Countess, who had, curiously enough, solicited their intervention, and freed her from the thraldom of an adulterous husband. It has been questioned whether the teachings and practice of the Scottish Protestants at that date gave liberty to the guilty parties to contract other unions after divorce. But it would appear that their doctrine on this point was still unsettled; that the Protestants of France from whom they derived their views left both divorce parties entirely free ; and that, practically, these French ideas prevailed among their congregations in our towns along the east coast. It may be true that the minister who subsequently married Bothwell to the Queen was deposed by the General Assembly for "marrying the divorcit adulterer". But this deposition only took place on the 30th December, 1567, when the Reformed divines had had time to discuss the question as they did without any result in the preceding June, and had adopted a provisional resolution to inhibit presently all ministers "to meddle with any sick marriages quhill full decision of the question". Thus Adam Bothwell was punished in virtue of an *ex-post-facto* enactment ; and when the Protestant Commissaries made their deliverance in favour of Jean Gordon, they were acting in accordance with their convictions at the time, and with the lights which they then possessed.

I am not called upon to enter into the motives which actuated Jean Gordon in lending herself to the institution of this double process. The young ladies of that period were schooled betimes into the utter sacrifice of their own wills to family interests, and it is reasonable to suppose that Jean did as she was bidden by the head of the house of Huntly. My business is with the attitude of the Queen—the Queen, indeed, by right of all the land, yet left at this crisis a victim to the untameable passions of a fiend in human form, and held in close durance by his myrmidons in Dunbar.

That Queen Mary was not guided by the motives gratuitously ascribed to her by hostile writers, in restoring freedom to the Archbishop's jurisdiction, is clear from the fact that the necessities of public business urged her to take that step, and that she revoked her sanction to it when it seemed likely to awaken religious discord and cause tumults in her capital. Moreover, no such formal restoration was required for any purpose that can be imagined; for the Archbishop, not believing that either Queen or Parliament could give or take away the authority with which he was invested, had continued to pronounce decisions in reference to marriages and the collation of benefices whenever he felt himself at freedom, notwithstanding the Act of the Parliament of 1560, which attempted to abolish the Papal supremacy in Scotland. For example, a sentence of divorce on the ground of nullity was published by his authority in the High Church of Glasgow, on the 30th of May, 1563. And, in point of fact, neither the Queen's approval nor her disapproval was taken into account, when, on the 7th May, 1566,

Bothwell and Lady Jean Gordon were declared to be unmarried.

The enemies of the Queen of Scots return to the assault, and reproach her with what they call "scandalous haste" in hurrying this double process to a conclusion. Now it cannot be denied that Bothwell and his abettors were eager enough to hasten the consummation of their iniquity. But there is evidence that the Queen had nothing to do with the instruction of the suits, and did not even know of their existence until they were far advanced. And besides, in the proceedings before either tribunal, we can discover no sign of haste on either case admitting of much cause for hesitation or for prolonged weighing of evidence. In a country where every man of any consequence was a born genealogist, and could commit his cousinships to the remotest degrees on his fingers' ends, it was not a very puzzling matter to discover whether the head of the great house of Bothwell was related within forbidden degrees to the sister of the head of the great house of Huntly. And if a dispensation had been obtained, Lady Jean's proctor and the judge-delegate had simply to examine, or cause to be examined, the entries in the books of the chancery of St. Andrews and the deanery of the Lothians.

Neither is there any "scandalous" or even undue haste visible in the proceedings of the Protestant tribunal. Earl James' evil propensities were as notorious throughout Scotland as his political and social position was eminent; and there is reason to believe that he never made the slightest attempt to play the sanctimonious Pharisee. The witnesses produced by Lady Jean were considered sufficient and irrefutable. And, as various writers observe, the lists presented to the Bench might have been indefinitely prolonged. There was little delay therefore in their deliberations, because none was required where doubt was altogether impossible. And the assertion that the Queen, influencing the processes, was guilty of "scandalous haste," is completely groundless, altogether gratuitous, and hurtful only to those who are reckless enough to maintain it. And finally, when Mary Stuart accepted the decision of her Council, that it was for her own honour and safety, for the welfare of her subjects and for the security of her Government, to marry James Hepburn, she cannot be accused of taking another woman's husband, since the two tribunals which represented all that was venerable and authorative in the eyes of all denominations among her people had solemnly dissolved the union between Bothwell and Lady Jean Gordon.

## Chapter X.

### John Craig and the Banns.

*An odious, a scandalous, and an infamous marriage.*
—Craig.

BOTHWELL'S ambitious designs could not brook delay. His confederates had plighted such faith and honour as they possessed, that he should have the hand of their Queen. But he knew how little they were trusted; and should the general public come at the true state of matters, commotions were certain to ensue. He immediately, therefore, took care to have his banns of marriage proclaimed in the High Church of Edinburgh, but in such a way as should merely fulfil the formalities exacted by law. John Knox had not yet had the courage to return to Edinburgh, and application had therefore to be made to John Craig.

General tradition gives celebrity to Craig's fortitude. Report had told him that the

Queen had been ravished, and was still in constraint. He considered Bothwell to be guilty of rape, adultery, and murder. Without a positive command signed by her Majesty, no such banns should be put up in his church. He is said to have carried his remonstrance to the hall where the Privy Council sat, to have reproached the Earl to his face with all his crimes, and to have taken heaven and earth to witness that he abhorred and detested such a marriage, as "odious and slanderous to the world," as "against all reason and good conscience," and offered to prove to them, by the Word of God, right reason, and good laws, that such a marriage was "scandalous and infamous".

I do not mean to diminish Craig's reputation for courage and zeal. From the time when he entered the Order of St. Dominic till he returned to his native country, Craig had occupied many positions, where he had valuable opportunities of mastering the sciences, sacred and profane. From the date of his appearing in the pulpits of Edinburgh, he might have acquired some knowledge of the people among whom he laboured, of the Court which he attended, and of the government of the realm and its administrators. But if we look narrowly into the line of conduct which he followed at this crisis of his sovereign's fate and fortunes, we find that his zeal wanted method and prudence, and his theology was inconsistent with his actions.

The proclamation of an intention to marry is not itself a marriage; it is a means prescribed by experience for the prevention of objectionable marriages. And Craig ought to have known that nothing could have been more serviceable at this juncture to his Queen than making known to all her subjects at home and her friends abroad the dreadful doom to which her treacherous Council were driving her. John Craig ought to have known, besides, that no power could, and, in the circumstances, no power should, have obliged him to publish the three banns all on one Sunday. Without giving sufficient delay to elicit objections, when there is good reasons to believe that objections may be forthcoming, the utility of banns in the public services of the Church altogether disappears. Now, when we consider what was the feverish agitation at this moment in the capital of Scotland, how eagerly events were watched from a distance, how rapidly new combinations were being formed among the nobles, how anxious friends were to aid Mary Stuart, if they only knew how, it is not too much to say that a fortnight's delay might have saved Scotland from a disgrace that will never be wiped out, and Scotland's Queen from an injury which she could never forget. It is clear, therefore, that John Craig's judgment and sagacity were sadly at fault. He resisted when he ought to have yielded, and yielded when he ought to have resisted. Moreover, when the hour of trial struck, John Craig did not display the courage of his convictions. A minister of religion who sanctions by his presence an "odious," a "scandalous," an "infamous" marriage has not in him the making of a martyr.

Before hastening on with the current of events, I must draw attention to the additional evidence which this incident affords of the complicity of the nobles with Bothwell's crimes. When Craig "discharged his conscience unto the Lords," we find it recorded that they "seemed unto him as so many slaves, what by flattery, what by silence, to give way to that abomination". And, again, we find him boldly affirming that "the best part of the realme did approve it ather be flatterie or be thair silence". These testimonies enable us to realise with what guilty obstinacy the Scottish Privy Council were determined to push their iniquity to its final consummation. Nothing would alter their resolution or arrest their progress. A man with whose depravity they were familiar, whose crimes they had shared, had dishonoured their Queen, and was detaining her in his unclean hands; and they approve his doings by their silence or flatter him openly and urge him forward. Nothing can more luminously demonstrate that they had made common cause with the new Duke of Orkney —new Lord of Shetland—in all his plans, his plottings, and his "abominations".

## Chapter XI.

### The Woful Wedding.

> Then come at once the lightning and the thunder,
> And distant echoes tell that all is rent asunder.
> —Old Play.

THE marriage is celebrated, and Mary Stuart has been forced to give her hand to Bothwell on the 13th May, 1567. The *Diurnal of Occurrents* speaks of it as a "marriage not *with the mass but with preaching*". (This form of speaking is now-a-days liable to misconception. By the *mass* and the *preaching*, people in the sixteenth century simply meant the Catholic and the Protestant religions. It is not, it never was, *essential* for a Catholic marriage that it should be celebrated during the Mass. And among Protestants a couple may be joined in wedlock without a sermon.) The *Diurnal* adds: "Neither pleasure nor pastime in it". So truly, I fear, thought the sorely tried Queen, for she is reported often to have said about this time that she wished only for death. Two days after the marriage, De Croc, the French Ambassador, reports that, "when closeted alone with Bothwell, Mary was heard to cry as loud as she could to give her a knife to kill herself. Those who were in the front room heard her. They thought that, if God did not help her, she would be driven to desperation. I have advised her and consoled her as much as I could," said De Croc. "He will not be long her husband; he is too much hated in this kingdom." Sir James Melville also says: "The Queen was so disdainfully handlet, and with sic reproachful language, that Arthur Aikin and I, being present, hard hir aske a knyfe to stick hirself, or ellis, said sche, I sall drowne myself". It is evident from these facts that Mary had no affection for Bothwell; and knowing this, the villain endeavoured to keep her down by ill-treatment. No common wrong could have wrung such words from Mary Stuart, but "not a day passed without brutish conduct on the husband's part and many a tear on hers". The marriage enabled the conspirators to assert with some plausibility Mary's complicity with Bothwell in Darnley's murder. I doubt whether the villains *counted beforehand* on Mary's marrying, or appearing to marry, Bothwell. If Mary had refused, they might have provoked the lecherous blackguard to do her unto death. But when Mary yielded so far, as I think she ought never to have done, the other course at once suggested itself to them. I think she should have run the risk of any dishonour rather than link herself, even in appearance, with such a profligate. But the ideas of that age, both in Scotland and in France, whence we drew all our laws and usages and ways of thinking, regarded subsequent marriage as the only possible reparation for abduction and dishonour. In many parts of Scotland the notion still prevails. That which was only whispered at the time of the King's death was openly written about now. The faction had engaged, with their partner in crime, that he should have that which he coveted most, the Queen; and they knew that when Mary could be made to marry Bothwell, it connected her with one of the murderers of her husband, and supplied material for a charge against both. James Hepburn, now Duke of Orkney, and royal consort, developed a most arrogant and overbearing disposition, and soon tried to play the King; but Mary had neither given him that title, nor the custody of her son, nor the keeping of the Castle of Stirling, where her son still remained under the care of the Earl of Mar.

Elizabeth's influence in Scotland, by an astute if niggardly administration of "comfort" in the shape of gold, was very considerable. She never liked Bothwell, and she liked him less now, posing as King, than as Scottish Commissioner on Border disputes. She had said, in a letter to Randolph, " In nowise, if we may choose, can we allow of Bothwell ". Mary married Bothwell on the 15th May, and on the 23rd Elizabeth wrote to Morton, telling him that " she could by no means allow of Bothwell," and she further told the Earl that he, and others like him, hirelings of hers, were to conduct themselves in a different way towards Bothwell to that in which they treated him " before and after Darnley's death ". This menace clearly meant the loss of their pensions, and therefore Morton and the others suddenly abandoned Bothwell, and went on the other tack. The Castle of Edinburgh was held by Sir James Balfour, a gentleman who, like Moray and others, was a sort of ecclesiastic. He was parish priest of Flisk, and, to put Church lands in his pocket, had always been ready for any piece of scoundrelism. Melville ingeniously tells us that he was at this time employed to corrupt Balfour, and he seems to have had little difficulty in getting this Protestant priest to join the confederacy against

Bothwell. The bond made with Balfour, which remains among the Morton papers, is of a very extraordinary character. In it he promises to aid the conspirators as commandant of Edinburgh Castle, if they take part with and defend him "in all his past actions". The murder of the King is here clearly meant. The conspirators further bind themselves to continue him in charge of the Castle, and to promote him when occasion arises; and Balfour, who knew what manner of men he was dealing with, stipulates that, in case " the nobility might alter on him," Grange should promise to be his protector. This most upright parson further stipulates, "to save his honour," that he was to be allowed to fire a shot or two towards them when they should first come to Edinburgh.

Bothwell had left his papers in the Castle of Edinburgh. Balfour broke open "a green desk" in which they were kept, and secured from among them "the principal band of the conspirators for Darnley's murder". They had Bothwell thus completely in their power; they could destroy the chief document proving their own guilt, or keep it concealed for their own use. The Castle of Edinburgh being shut against him, the new Duke of Orkney escaped with the Queen, and levied such force in her name as he could, but the rumours that he had ravished the Queen and was holding her by force deprived the royal proclamations of their authority. Morton, Kirkcaldy, and the others collected men, and Hume advanced on Borthwick Castle, but "her Majestie in mennis claithes, butit and spurit, depairted that samin nicht from Borthwick to Dunbar". On the 15th June, on Carberry Hill, the two forces met. The Queen had some 2000 men; "the best pairt was commons". Her enemies had 1800 horsemen and 400 footmen, all gentlemen "in their gaire". While the parties stood facing each other, De Croc, the aged Ambassador of France, tried to effect a reconciliation. "He assured them on the part of the Queen that she was anxious to prevent the shedding of blood, and eager to favour peace. To effect these objects she would grant them pardon, and declare a general oblivion of what had been done." To this Morton, in the name of the confederates, said: "We came not here to fight against the Queen, but against the murderers of the King!" The fanatic Glencairn added: "We came not to ask pardon, but to grant it to some who have offended". What did this idiot mean? Did he insinuate that they had come in arms to Carberry to grant pardon to Bothwell? The French Ambassador, seeing how things were likely to go, left the field and returned to Edinburgh.

Bothwell then sent a herald into the hostile camp offering to prove his innocence by single combat. James Murray of Tullibardine offered to accept the challenge, but Bothwell naturally declined to cross swords with an inferior in rank. He openly challenged Morton, who accepted, and named two-handed swords as weapons. The conflict to be on foot. Lord Lindsay, at this point, begged to be allowed to fight for Morton, but the Queen interfered. How much it is to be regretted that she did not allow the fight to come on between these two convicted murderers of the King. As Chalmers says, "the best consummation had been that they had killed one another, for they were two of the most guilty men on earth". The Queen then sent for the Laird of Grange, who was reputed the best soldier in Scotland, and more honest than his comrades who were always leading him by the nose. He came fully empowered by the rebel chiefs to come to terms of reconciliation for them and for himself. He proposed that, as Bothwell was suspected of the King's murder, he should pass off the field until the cause might be tried, and that the Queen should pass over to them and take the counsel of her nobles. They, in return, would honour, serve, and obey her Majesty as their sovereign. To this proposal the Queen agreed. Grange thereupon took Bothwell by the hand and urged him to depart. Rather a strange method of bringing to justice the man whom they declared to be the chief murderer of the King! A curious termination of a campaign expressly undertaken to pursue, apprehend, and punish Bothwell! They catch their man and let him off, and promise not to follow him! Grange undertook that if the Earl, now Duke, the husband whom just a month before they had forced upon their Queen, went his way, no one would hinder him, and the brutish fellow went. He went, leaving her he had so grossly wronged to the tender care of a band of men, unscrupulous, hypocritical, capable of atrocities as great as his own. "Madam," said Morton, as he took the Queen over to the rebel force, "here is the place where your Grace should be. We will honour, serve, and obey you, as ever the nobility of this realm did your pregenitors." Oh! most splendid promise! Oh! most solemn mockery!

How did Morton fulfil this promise solemnly made on the field of battle? He carried Mary, about seven o'clock in the evening, to the house of the Provost of Edinburgh, weeping sorely, surrounded by an insulting crowd, "while before her watery eyes," as Chalmers puts it, he, a murderer by his own avowal, had the effrontery "to display a banner of white taffety, on which was painted a representation of the strangled King with the young Prince on his knees, crying out, "Judge and avenge my cause, O Lord!" This banner could not have been got ready on the spur of the moment. To embroider or to paint it must have taken some time. And it is of itself an evidence of forethought, premeditation, and *malice prepense*. While it was being got ready, they were solemnly promising to honour, serve, and obey the poor Queen! Little rest had Mary Stuart in the Provost's house that first night. The refuse of the town purposely collected, howled and yelled round the building until morning, and the first sight that met Mary's eyes was that brutal banner fluttering in the breeze before her window. The yells of the crowd and the sight of that vile flag inflicted on the agonised Queen sorrow enough, but sadder sorrow must have crept upon her as she thought of the new proof she had of the perfidy of her nobles —men, as Chalmers says, "who had no religion, or morals, or honour, or good faith"; and if there came to Mary consolation at all, it came to her from her conscious innocence and well-balanced faith. The perfidy of Morton and his gang in treating Mary as they did was likely to rouse into activity the liking for her which the craftsmen and better class of citizens ever had ; and to prevent a rising which was imminent, Morton next day caused it to be made known that they were protecting the Queen from insult and restoring her to freedom. Next day showed what these men meant by protection, and what freedom they thought their sovereign should enjoy.

## Chapter XII.

### Not Holyrood, But Lochleven.

> 'Tis a weary life this—
> Vaults overhead, and grates and bars around.
> —The Woodsman.

ON the afternoon of the 16th June the Queen was taken to her Palace of Holyrood, but neither freedom nor state were restored to her.

In vain did Mary give instructions to that most unworthy secretary of hers "to convene the Estates of the realm, as she was willing to submit to their determination, she being present and heard". When darkness had set in, they took Mary a prisoner to the Castle of Lochleven, duping the Laird of Grange by producing a pretended letter of the Queen's to Bothwell. This letter was never produced again. "The Queen has offered her cause," says the Bishop of Ross, "to the decision of the Estates, but God knoweth, it is all in vain, for they have now obtained their prey."

Where was the brutal cause of all this trouble—Bothwell? His execrable crimes were the immediate cause of the unspeakable misery into which the woman was plunged, whom he had forced to be his wife. He had taken her advice at Carberry Hill, he had "loupit on his horse and ridden to Dunbar," and there, in the comfort of his castle, did he think of her whom he had ruined for ever. That he really loved Mary is doubtful. That he was aware that Mary did *not* love him is certain. The story of her readiness to follow him in a white petticoat is one of those monstrous inventions which are a special feature of the period. Knowledge of the man keeps charity back from believing that this true scion of the race of Hepburn troubled himself much about the fate of his victim.

On reaching the Castle of Lochleven we get a further evidence of the ingenious malice of these rebel lords. The keeper of the castle was Sir William Douglas, whose mother was the frail lady who in other years had borne to Mary's father that ill-omened son whom Mary's generosity had enriched and made Earl of Moray. Sir William Douglas was thus Moray's half-brother. Robert Douglas, William's father, had married Meg Erskine with her shattered fame.

Sir William was the Earl of Morton's presumptive heir, and in later years actually succeeded to the title. The selection of the Castle of Lochleven as a prison for Queen Mary throws a vivid light on the connections and dealings of this clique of Douglases with their base kinsman the Earl of Moray. Moray availed himself of his kinship to keep Morton steady to his interests, and we shall see him for the same reason trusting to the fidelity of the keeper of Lochleven. He acted now as he had done, when he took advantage of their connection with Darnley, whose mother was a Douglas, to entrap the giddy and passionate young King into Riccio's murder.

Of course Dame Douglas ceased not to comfort the crushed and captive Queen with tales of the legitimacy of her son, she herself being Mary's father's wife, and so on—a singularly ingenious way of giving pain, to place this aged harridan in charge of Scotland's Queen!

This state of matters continued until the end of May, by which time threats of death had enabled the nobles to force from Mary renunciation of the crown in favour of her son, making the unscrupulous half-brother of her keeper Regent. The nobles carried the infamy of the deed as far as cruellest mockery could do, by bringing to the imprisoned Queen two notaries, who got her, while signing the enforced demission, to protest that she was not a prisoner. The warrant for Mary's imprisonment in Lochleven Castle had the signatures of Morton, Athole, Glencairn, Mar, Graham, and Sanquhar attached to it. Yet these men say that, after mature consultation, "it is thocht convenient, concludit, and decernit that her Majesty's person be sequestret from all society of Earl Bothwell, and ordains the Queen to be conveyed to Lochleven, and kepit surely, and no lerand person is to get intelligence from her except bi directions of the lords underscriband". Mary's friends protested against the usage given, and refused to recognise her resignation of the crown, forced from her under such conditions. The General Assembly even issued an address and demanded that the cause of the Queen's detention should be explained, or that she should be set at liberty. The conspirators had, however, gone too far to recede; so, acting as a Council of Government, they adopted a course that must have appeared to other nations amazing. They charged Mary with the murder of Darnley. What would Englishmen have said if Cecil and Walsingham had charged Elizabeth with adultery and murder? But as Mr. Caird says, "There was great difficulty in the way. That double traitor Balfour still held the Castle of Edinburgh, and kept his grip of the bond against Darnley. It was necessary to buy him a second time. The wily parson of Flisk stood out for an exorbitant price;" and that price, great as it was, was paid.

On the 8th December, Mary Stuart would have completed her 25th year. Disputes have been raised about the exact date of Mary's birth. I think that she was born either on the 7th in the evening, or the 8th in the morning. The 8th, from 1st Vespers on the 7th, was the Feast of the Conception of Our Ladye, a circumstance which doubtless had its share in determining her name. Mary's power to revoke those grants already spoken of would expire by law on that day. She conceived that the Parliamentary sanction obtained only removed the statutory nullity attaching to Crown grants made without Parliamentary sanction. She had still, then, her private right of revocation on the ground of minority. She had before this date executed secretly a partial revocation. This fact again excited the alarm of the holders of these lands, and Mary's friends boasted of what this revocation would do.

The rebel lords could not go before Parliament with things in that state. They therefore came to Balfour's terms, and got from him in return "the writings, which did comprehend the names and consents of the chiefs for the murdering of the King". The Earl of Moray conveyed to Balfour for this "Bond" the Priory of Pittenweem, £5000 in money, remission for his connection with the King's murder, and a pension to his son, a deed which is irrefragable evidence of Moray's complicity in Darnley's murder, and all the subsequent doings of the confederates. The new Prior of Pittenweem then gave up the castle of his Queen to the handling of her rebel lords, and "the Bond" criminating these rebels so directly was, we are told, in a letter of one of the English Ministers, at the hands of Lethington, "turned into ashes". The insurgent nobles, Chalmers says, "seized the Queen's plate, jewels, and other movables in Holyrood House"—amongst other things, a Silver Casket, the gift of Francis, in happier years, to his now suffering Mary. Glencairn went with his servants into the chapel and broke down the altars, and demolished the pictures, images, and ornaments. This destruction of other people's property was highly commended by the preachers, as a mark of great godliness!

Bothwell had meanwhile left the Castle of Dunbar in charge of his depute, the laird of

Whitelaw, and put to sea in two small vessels. Bothwell's real purpose was probably to go by Orkney, Denmark, and Germany to France, to endeavour to raise friends and money for his own cause, and, perhaps, for that of the hapless lady whom he declared to be his wife. He and his followers went, however, no further at first than the palace of Spynie in Moray, the house of his grand-uncle, Bishop Patrick Hepburn. Futile and inconsistent proclamations* in the name of the Queen had been issued against him by the insurgents, who might, if they had chosen, have kept him in their clutches at Carberry or blockaded him at Dunbar. Two ships were now sent after him, under charge of Grange and Tullybardin, but Bothwell managed in Orkney and in Shetland to avoid them, and escape as easily as he had done at Dunbar. Among the islands he lost one of his little ships. In the tortuous navigation of the Sound of Bressay he caused his enemies to lose their best ship. Sailing towards Norway, he attempted the capture of a trading vessel somewhere on the coast. The Danish Government at once sent vessels of war against him, his vessel was seized, and he and his crew put in prison; there, in the meantime, we may leave the Lord High Admiral of Scotland a prisoner, richly meriting what fate had sent him.

## Chapter XIII.

### The Silver Casket.

> Contained the only proof that Moray, Morton, and Lennox did ever pretend to have against the Queen.
> —GOODALL.

WE are now arrived, says the trustworthy Chalmers, at the 20th June, 1567, "the epoch of the supposed discovery of a boxful of letters—love letters from the Queen to Bothwell—from a married woman to a married man—from a wife who wished to save her husband to a conspirator who was leagued to murder him". And this box, the afterwards famous Silver Casket, was said to have been seized, and taken from George Dalgleish, a servant of Bothwell's, by Morton. Sir James Balfour, keeper of the Castle, gave it, they said, to Dalgleish to take to Bothwell at Dunbar. The Lords of the Secret Council examined this man six days after on a charge of his being one of Darnley's murderers. Of the so-called interceptor of the box, Morton, they asked not a single question as to Casket and letters! The Casket was evidently an after-thought to make a story in London. Valiant and true-hearted Scots! who accuse the descendant of the ancient kings before a—what?—on the English throne. Nor is there in all the consultations held by the insurgent nobles between 26th June and 4th December one single allusion to the Casket or its contents; nor have we in the bond for crowning the Queen's son and supporting his government any insinuation of the existence of such a criminating mass of evidence against the Queen; but, instead of this, we have this entry of the 26th June: "The Lords have, by evident proof, as well of witness as writing, made manifest to them that James Earl of Bothwell was the principal adviser of the murder, and was at the actual doing thereof himself"; and on the 9th and 21st July the Privy Council minutes tell us: "That said Earl did, first, treasonably ravish her Majesty's most nobill person, and then constrainit hir—being in his bondage and thraldom—to contract sic a pretendit and unlawful marriage with him".

Is it likely that such entries as these would have been made with the Silver Casket and the letters in their hands? These men, Morton, Glencairn, Maitland, Mar, or Graham, were they likely to hold back from using such an instrument? But the truth is the forged papers had not then been created. Balfour and Maitland were shaping out an entire lie from a divided truth. Amongst Darnley's papers, which they destroyed, were two affectionate loving letters of the Queen to him, not dated, and not addressed. These they kept. Amongst the list of Mary's property at Holyrood, they found a Silver Casket. They did not turn into coin that casket as they did the plate, &c. They kept it, as they had kept the two letters found among Darnley's papers. Lethington's wife wrote amazingly like Mary. By a forged paper they had already sent Mary into Lochleven; by a few forged love letters from Mary to Bothwell these two ingenious lawyers could piece out their case. We know it was pieced out, and coarse men coined other letters to be used with bits of the forged ones and the sonnets, as if all were Mary's.

The writers of the letters made no attempt to make the substance of these vile letters in any way, other than the form of writing, to correspond with Mary's style. They read liker what "fat Jack" would have said, not written, to Dame Quickly, as he sat by her seacoal fire, and there too freely used the parcel-gilt goblet. All Mary's real correspondence—and there is a great wealth of it—is, as Mr. Caird says, "everywhere imbued with the noblest feelings, the purest language, the purest thought, pity and mercy on every page". Would Mary, in writing to Bothwell, have expressed her desire to be joined to him in wedlock by any such expression as "We are coupled with a false race, the devil sinder us, and God knit us together for ever"? That "horrible and long letter," which Elizabeth's Commissioner speaks of, is the one of the set which proves the forgery best. "Four-fifths of it consist of a curt and business-like recital of circumstances such as would have been proper for the Queen to state in a memorial for the information of her Privy Council. But there are at the commencement, towards the middle, and at the end passages of the most extravagant love-making and palpable suggestions of murder—passages so different in style, language, and thought from the rest of the paper, that one cannot understand how they could have come from the same mind."

Not certainly from the mind of Mary Stuart, the most accomplished lady of her time. The interpolations in the beginning, middle, and end of this "horrible and long letter" were "scribbled in Scotch". This letter, as produced by the conspirators, was wholly in French. It was critically examined by Goodall and the elder Tytler, and proved by them to be not the original, but a translation; that the translation was from Buchanan's Latin; and that Buchanan's Latin was itself the translation of Moray's Scotch. One amusing instance is given by Goodall. The Scotch version makes the Queen say, "I am irkit and goin' to sleep". It was for some time questioned whether Queen Mary could speak "Scots". This question appears to be settled by a letter of the Father Nicholas de Gouda, published a few years ago in a German periodical. It is there stated that she conversed in Scots with Edmond Hay. We are thus led to infer that she, the Maries, and her other Scottish attendants kept up their native tongue in France. But whether she could *write* it before the solitude of her weary imprisonment in England gave her time for study is another question. Of the several languages with which she became acquainted during her life, she had most command of the French. Up till 1562, she could understand Latin when spoken to her, but could not speak it easily enough to maintain a conversation. There is a great deal of nonsense in history about people knowing *perfectly* a *great* number of languages. To resume our analysis of the letters. Was it failing eyesight, or a falling tear,

or a muddled brain, that made our old scholar read "nakit" for "irkit," *i.e.*, weary, and solemnly render that into "Ego nudata sum"? The French translator improves upon Buchanan, and writes "toute nue" (stark nakit). Caird says truly, "A strange condition for her Majesty while writing so long a letter, in a northern January". Surely all will agree with Dr. Samuel Johnson, who, forgetful that a slander has as many lives as a cat, declared "that the Silver Casket letters were spurious, and would never again be brought forward as historic evidence". Boswell's hero forgot that few men have patience to go down to the bottom of the deep well where truth lies, and there hide themselves from the prejudices that fill the upper air.

On the 4th December, the Regent and his Council forged and forwarded to Englan dan Act of Council in which they charge the Queen not only with the murder of her husband, but with an intent to murder her child! Three of the known murderers of the King signed this Act—Morton, Maitland, and Balfour—as may be seen in Haynes' collection. But the Register of the Scottish Privy Council contains no such Act. It was simply an imposition practised on Elizabeth's ministers. In it they justify the *imprisonment of the Queen* (but why in Lochleven?) by the evidence of her guilt which her letters to Bothwell disclose, yet these men admit that the letters did not fall into their hands until some time after Mary had been made a prisoner. The conduct of the Regent in accusing his sister to a foreign government of the most atrocious crimes, and the unprecedented severities which he inflicted, made him unpopular. " Great dissatisfaction continued to be expressed that the murderers of the King remained unpunished." In order apparently to silence these murmurs, he had four wretched subordinates who had no will of their own, brought to trial for Darnley's murder. With indecent haste the four— Hay, Hepburn, Nicholas Hubert (commonly called Paris), and Dalgleish—were condemned and executed. Paris and Dalgleish by-and-by figure in the fiction of the find of the Silver Casket and letters; but dead men tell no tales. The declarations of Hay and Hepburn on the scaffold implicated many nobles, and deepened the popular growl of discontent. Moray began to see other perils threatening him like lurid clouds. Maitland, long accustomed to lead, grew weary of the second place, and the Regent knew that at any moment he might turn against him. The Scottish nobles of that age were indeed always turning against each other. If Moray had given them time, they would have all combined against him, and given us a new chapter of revelations. But Bothwellhaugh's blunderbuss unfortunately prevented us from getting at a deal of that truth which honest men learn when rogues fall out. Fleming held Dumbarton for the Queen. Huntly, Argyle, and others barely acknowledged the Regent. The Hamiltons of course hated him, because they suspected he had designs upon the crown, which they hoped would soon be theirs.

Sensible of his gathering dangers, Moray sought the help of his old ally, the Queen of England. To London, then, the Regent sent Nicolas Elphinstone with a copy of his Act, in which he charged his sister with having murdered her husband and tried to murder her son. Being scarce of money, he sent with Elphinstone Mary's jewels to offer to Elizabeth for sale! Dr. Joseph Robertson, in his preface to *The History of Queen Mary's Jewels*, says: "There were one hundred and eighty entries, or twenty-one more than the inventory made at her departure from France. Among the articles added we may recognise a cross of gold set with diamonds and rubies, which Mary had lately redeemed from the hands in which it was pledged by her mother for a thousand pounds. Another acquisition is of pearls, which, as they were bought from an Edinburgh goldsmith, we may perhaps presume to be Scottish." Mary had given her brother charge of these jewels on one of his visits to her at Lochleven. But James's greed could never resist temptation. And no wonder that many folk believed that Meg Erskine's son had not a drop of Stuart blood in his veins. His manner of reforming the Church was to eat up fat prebends, to send all the brass and copper of the altars, choir-stalls, and other furniture of the churches over to Holland for sale. He professed unwillingness, yet accepts the trust of his sister's jewels, and then sends them to market. When the Parliament met he took good care to get an Act of Indemnity for his intromissions with his sister's jewels. At his death some of the most valuable of them were in the possession of his wife. Elizabeth helped him little in his troubles with the management of Scottish affairs, but she helped herself to the bribe he laid before her—Mary's pearls, at the price of 12,000 crowns. They were said to be the finest pearls in Europe, and were worth very much more, as the vain and parsimonious Elizabeth had discreetly ascertained.

Disappointed with Elizabeth, the Regent next applied for help to the King of France, Charles

IX., but without success, the French Ambassador having warned his Sovereign that two-thirds of the people of Scotland were ready to rise against Moray and his faction. The enemies of the Regent, he adds, have two objects in view—the first, "to liberate the Queen; the second, that the Regent, Lethington, and others clear themselves of the murder of the late King of Scotland". Is it not curious to observe how the popular instinct swerved not from the suspicion of the guilt of the Moray faction? In closest durance Mary had spent the winter at Lochleven, but Mary Seton, Jane Kennedy, and Marie Courcelles shared her captivity, and they jointly shaped an effort to gain for their Queen her freedom, and the opportunity of testing the soundness of the French Ambassador's estimate of her people's wishes. By the help of Willie Douglas, page to the lady of Lochleven, on Sunday evening, 2nd May, 1568, a postern gate close to the water's edge was opened, and there a boat lay waiting, into which the Queen, in the dress of Mary Seton, stepped with two of her attendants. There are various versions of the manner of Mary's escape. Looking back now, it may be said that her escape was premature: her loyal subjects were not yet ready; their plans were not finally drawn out. On the other hand, every day the ill-will against Moray was increasing, and within a few months would have ripened into revolt. Mary was quickly rowed to the western shore, where Lord Seton, with a small body of horsemen, awaited her coming. At utmost speed he took her to his Castle of Niddry, in West Lothian.

## Chapter XIV.

### Queen once more.

*No chieftain there rode half so free,
Or half so light and gracefullie.
'Twas sweet to see her ringlets pale
Wide waving in the southlan' gale!*
—Hogg.

NEXT morning the Queen reached Hamilton, where, in a very few days, she found herself at the head of an army of 6000 men.

Mr. Hosack, at this date, remarks: "The staunchest supporters of the Queen were Protestant nobles. No circumstance in the life of Mary Stuart is more remarkable than that, in spite of all the efforts of Moray and his faction, this was so"—Moray's "evangel" was place and mammon. An application made by him to *France* shows that he was quite ready to return to the old religion if he had any sort of certainty that the change would have answered his schemes. Had he lived to see Henry IV. of France *twice* converted to the faith of his fathers, he might have cleverly followed the example. Sincere men were scarce in that generation; yet in spite of all the violence of the preachers, she, the Catholic Queen of Scotland, daughter of the hated house of Guise, the reputed mortal enemy of their religion, did now, after being maligned as the most abandoned of her sex, find her best friends among her Protestant subjects. This appears at first sight inexplicable. A phenomenon so strange admits of only one explanation. If throughout her reign Mary had not loyally kept her promises of security and toleration to her Protestant subjects, they assuredly, in her time of need, would not have risked in her defence their lives and fortunes.

The Regent had a force at his command, scarcely strong enough to warrant an attack upon the Queen's adherents. She made an injudicious effort to prevent bloodshed, and gave him time. The Regent, having tasted power, was determined to make an effort to keep it. Knowing that the Hamiltons, who had long been kept in the background, were cold in the Queen's service, and that the Earl of Huntly was on his way with a force to join Mary, he struck at once, trusting to the military skill of Kirkcaldy of Grange. The fight at Langside proved ruinous to the Queen.

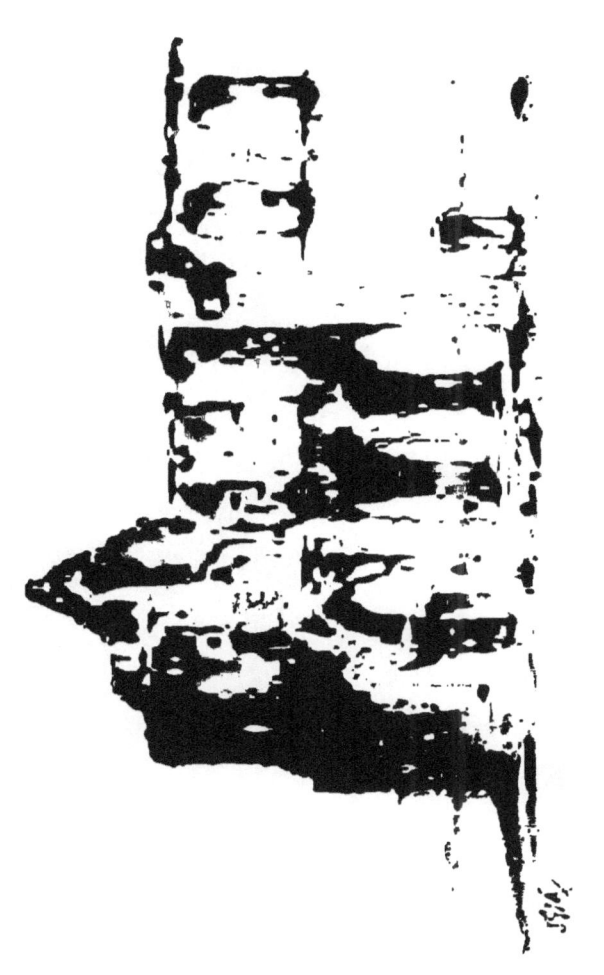

She might, if she had been less hemmed in by her foes, have found shelter in Dumbarton Castle. By the advice of Lord Herries, however, she made for Galloway, and never drew bridle until she reached the shelter of the Abbey of Dundrennan, full sixty miles away from the field of her last battle.

In the Abbey, the few friends who had shared her rapid flight assembled in consultation. Queen Elizabeth had repeatedly invited Mary to come to her should she ever escape from the walls of Lochleven and need a place of refuge. Elizabeth had promised to meet her in person, and give her such a reception in England as was due to a queen, a kinswoman, and an ally. Mary, enfeebled by her long imprisonment, never dreamt that she was going to another, longer, drearier, and more unendurable. She could not see through the character of her royal cousin, and never profited by the frequent lessons she had received. She was on the frontier of England, and resolved to try her fortune on the farther shore of the Solway. It took nineteen years of cruel usage to convince Mary of the wickedness and mendacity of her fair-spoken cousin.

## Chapter XV.

### Into England.

> Scotland's sae fu' o' treacherie
> Fae highest estate to lowest degree,
> That nivir a man daur lift a han'
> For his queen and countrie.
> —*Old Ballad.*

MEANWHILE, I think, before we follow Mary into England, we should give, while yet in the land of her birth, the further evidence of her entire innocence of the heaviest of the charges which her enemies have laid against her. Her reluctant marriage with Bothwell gave the only likely colour to it at the time, and ten years after that scoundrel Earl made solemn oath that Mary knew nought whatever of the deed. At the very time that Bothwell, in Danish prison cell, and near his end, was making this statement, the mother of the murdered King was writing to Mary in the most affectionate terms. In one of her letters quoted by Miss Strickland the noble lady says: "I beseech

your Majesty, fear not, but trust in God that all shall be well. The treachery of your traitors is known better than before. I shall always play my part to your Majesty's content." Did the mother of the King think —as she probably at first believed—that Mary was his murderer? Lastly, and little though it seem, there is significant meaning in the finding among Mary's relics, which honest Elizabeth took from her at Chartley, miniatures of Francis the Second, miniatures of Darnley, of Mary and Darnley, and of Mary, Darnley, and their son in one jointed set of gold frames, but neither miniature, nor ring, nor letter, nor anything to indicate James Hepburn.

In the imprisonment at Lochleven Mary had often received in writing from Elizabeth assurances of hospitality and protection. In one instance a diamond ring was sent to Mary as a token of this friendship. Relying on these promises, and in opposition to much remonstrance, Mary crossed the Solway on the 16th May, 1568, in a small boat, and landed at Workington. " For ninety miles," writes Mary, " I rode across the country without lightin' or drawin' bridle; slept on the bare floor; no food but oatmeal, without the company of a female, not daring to travel except by stealth at night."

Three of her devoted Scottish nobles, Lords Herries, Livingstone, and Fleming, all Protestants, went with her. Lord Scrope, the warden of the Western Marches, was in London when Mary entered on English soil. His deputy, Mr. Lowther, however, received her with all due respect, and, accompanied by several gentlemen of Cumberland, attended her to Carlisle. Never thinking of Elizabeth's jealous nature, Mary wrote in praise of Lowther's attention and care. Elizabeth showed her estimate by laying on Lowther a fine, which, to pay, caused him to sell two of his estates! Mr. Hosack tells us Cecil knew well the value of having Mary personally in his power. She was already, as Mr. Hosack says, "a prisoner, and the utmost precautions were forthwith taken to prevent her escape". Cecil, writing with his own hand: "The surety of the Queen of Scots is first to be considered, that by no practice she should be conveyed out of the realm".

It was not known until the 20th June that Elizabeth's objections to Cecil's proposed treatment of Mary had their way. On that day the Council of Ministers resolved to summon Mary from Carlisle, it being too near the Border. It was further resolved that the Queen of England should proceed to be informed of the cause between the Queen of Scots and her subjects. The document then proceeds to speak of the danger of allowing Mary to proceed to France, of her not having signed the treaty of Edinburgh, of her having married her late husband, a subject of Elizabeth, without Elizabeth's consent, and then the paper concludes with the following significant sentences: "That neither the Queen's Majesty, with honour or surety to herself, nor yet with quietness to the realm, give the Queen of Scots aid, nor permit her to come to her presence. Nor to be restored. Nor to depart the realm before her cause be honourably tried." By whom? Where were now Elizabeth's friendly promises? What a future was here prepared for England! "Nineteen years," says Mr. Hosack, " of successive insurrections, and conspiracies, and plots. Nineteen years of incessant remonstrances, anxiety, danger, and recrimination, quenched in blood, and followed by an eternity of infamy. It is well for mankind that acts of national injustice should rarely pass unpunished; and never did a political crime entail a heavier measure of retribution than did the keeping captive and then murdering Mary Queen of Scots."

As far as reigning and ruling over Scotland

is concerned, Mary's name no longer floats on the mid-stream of Scottish story. In very deed she is Elizabeth's prisoner. The faith she resolutely holds is not so much unpopular as beaten down by a triumphant faction. Many events show that those classes of the population who had nothing to gain by the revolution were still attached to their old faith. This was quite natural for a stubborn and opinionative race like the Scots. Unfortunately, there was no portion of the population of Scotland in the sixteenth century that really deserved the title of "people" as we employ the word now-a-days. The vassals of the great chiefs and lords were not supposed to have minds or consciences independent of their superiors; and the heritable jurisdictions proved an efficacious means for enforcing conformity in politics and religion. "Dinna anger the laird" was the maxim that justified every course of action. The laird's feud and the laird's religion, the laird's king and the laird's party, were every vassal's watchword and every vassal's safety. There was no class distinct from the lairds and their immediate kindred who had any influence or power to make that influence felt. At the present day, with our freedom of discussion, our newspapers, and our public spirit, a revolution, like that which took place under Mary, would be utterly impossible. There is a Scottish people now, and they would not submit to be led by men like Moray, Morton, Maitland, and Ruthven. Mary's attachment to her creed and to her country may have largely helped to ruin both. Had she listened to John Knox the wealth of the Church might have been more readily kept out of lay hands, and she herself might have ruled in greater quiet. Yet it is more probable, if she had adopted the tenets of the Reformer, swarms of hornets would have assailed her from every parish where there was an acre of secularised property. Had she owned the supremacy of England, and given to Elizabeth the feudal homage that Baliol gave to Edward, though it might not have silenced a vain and jealous woman, it would have flattered and pleased a powerful Queen. The daughter of that Defender of the Faith to whom England's newer form of godliness had been great gain found much in the new order of things to comfort her. Mary Stuart found nothing but avarice and falsehood under a cloak of religion everywhere. It has been well said, that "if Elizabeth had pursued a straightforward course when Mary fell into her hands, much evil might have been spared". Had Elizabeth had the courage and generosity to set Mary free, Mary might have gone to France or Spain, married a foreigner, and thus lost the sympathies of the English and the Scottish Catholics; but, retaining Mary as a prisoner, Elizabeth gave cause for no end of conspiracies. Elizabeth reigned over England as many years as Mary was allowed to live. Elizabeth had ruled England for ten years when the Queen of Scots, trusting to Elizabeth's repeated proffers of protection and help, went into the most complete imprisonment and torment that one woman could invent against another woman whose wit and beauty she envied.

The points of contrast between Mary and Elizabeth are curiously humorous. They both were fond of dancing. Mary danced well; Elizabeth grotesquely. They were both sensible to the attractions of handsome manhood. Mary married early; Elizabeth pretended that she never meant to marry, yet on to a grey old age she ever kept a lover to whisper soft ditties in her ear, and the catalogue of her sweethearts is only now in our days being completed by industrious research. Mary was warm-hearted and generous; Elizabeth cold, cruel, and vindictive. She caused the right hand of a man to be struck off because he had written against her marrying the Duke of Alençon, and she joked when she heard of the execution of her lover Seymour. Mary's attendants loved her, Elizabeth's feared her; Mary's language and thoughts were pure, generous even to weakness, and refined; the Tudor Queen tickled Leicester in the neck, even in the presence of an Ambassador, and cursed and swore like any trooper. The Bishop of Aquila says that she undertook to do what she did at the bidding of her sister Mary—become a Roman Catholic—if Philip of Spain would support her on the throne if she became the wife of Leicester. An endless set of contrasts might be brought together, but these are sufficient to show what the two Queens were as women. Mary, therefore, had a conscience, though in some matters of lesser importance she was not always faithful to it. Elizabeth was ready to sacrifice soul and body to save her skin or gratify her likings. And we must not omit to remark, that while no one could reproach Mary with a single act of ingratitude, the life of Elizabeth is full of such. More than once she owed her life to Philip; what of her gratefulness? Elizabeth sent a letter of condolence to Mary, but refused to see her. She instructed Lord Scrope and Sir Francis Knollys strictly to watch her, and when Mary pled as an independent sovereign for some other usage than this, Elizabeth's representatives wrote to their mistress: "We found hyr in hyr answers to have an eloquent tongue and a discreet heid, and it seemeth by hyr doings that she hath stoute courage and liberalle harte adjoined thereunto".

Mary's dignified attitude, the eloquence of her language, the keenness of her judgment, the courage she displayed under her reverses, made a deep impression on the English envoys. On seeing the hopeless nature of her communications with Elizabeth's representatives, Mary sent to London two of her own most trusted adherents, Earls Fleming and Herries, to negotiate a loan for her on the security of her income as Dowager-Queen of France. They were the bearers of a letter also from Mary to Elizabeth, urgently seeking an interview, that she might make known her wrongs and vindicate her character. The wily Elizabeth yielded to none of Mary's requests, yet gave no decided refusal, adroitly seizing Mary's desire to exculpate herself as evidence of Mary's acknowledgment of Elizabeth's jurisdiction. The Regent sent from Scotland something very like an acknowledgment on the part of himself and his rebellious faction to accept Elizabeth as judge in the quarrel between them and their Queen. Artfully Elizabeth turned this to her own account, and, changing an offer of explanation into a defence, she resolved to constrain Mary to prove her innocence of Darnley's murder, and the Regent to free himself of the charge of rebellion, pretending at the same time that her only object in accepting the office of arbitrator was her desire to get an opportunity of reconciling them to each other. Neither Fleming nor Herries was satisfied, and when Herries asked Elizabeth, as she would not grant a personal interview to Mary, to allow her leave to quit England and return to Scotland in the little boat in which she came, or to go to France, if not to Scotland, " No," said Elizabeth, " I will not prove myself so imprudent as to permit this, and be held in low esteem among other princes. When Mary was there in France before, the King, her husband [but he was now dead, and as far as that goes there should have been no hindrance to letting Mary go], assumed for her the title and arms belonging to my crown, though I was then alive, and I will not again place myself in such embarrassing circumstances. As to her return to Scotland in the humble conveyance you have mentioned, since she has come into my country, it would neither be to her honour nor to mine for her to go back; besides, it would not be for her advantage to do so." What insolent hypocrisy!! Elizabeth would take better care of Mary than Mary would of herself!!!

Elizabeth then sent Mr. Middlemore into Scotland to inform Moray of her desire to arbitrate, at the same time commanding the Regent to cease the war he was waging in Scotland against his enemies. At the head of an army of six thousand men, he was "enforcing obedience to the young King," and Elizabeth sagely enough said that what the Regent was doing " sounds very strange in the ear of us, being a Prince Sovereign having dominions and subjects committed to our power as your Queen had". Middlemore on his way to Scotland called on Mary at Carlisle, on the 13th June, and is reported to have, among other insulting utterances, said to Mary that his mistress could not see her until she proved herself innocent of Darnley's murder. Mary, indignant at such language, demanded— "Am I a prisoner?" "No," said Elizabeth's representative, "but I am instructed to dissuade you from going into Scotland or seeking an interview with the Queen of England," but to "wait her judgment, and you will then see with what love, with what heart, with what joy, if found innocent, her Majesty will receive you, embrace you, and do everything for you that you could desire". At the words " judgment" and "trial" Mary indignantly said, "I have no other judge but God; none other can take upon themselves to judge me. I offered, of my own free will, according to the good trust I reposed in the Queen my sister, to make her judge of my cause. But how can that be, when she will not suffer me to come to her?"

Mary then demanded to be admitted to an interview with Elizabeth, or to be promptly supplied with assistance, or to be permitted to go elsewhere to obtain the means of returning to her kingdom. In the pathetic letter which she wrote to Elizabeth, Mary says: "Remove from your mind, madam, the idea that I came here for the preservation of my life, for neither the world nor the whole of Scotland have rejected me. I came to regain my honour and to chastise my false accusers. I chose you in preference to all other princes, as being my nearest relation and staunch friend [Mary's penetration was not great], doing you, as I supposed, an honour. I neither can nor will reply to the false accusations of my subjects, and justify myself as a dependent before them. They and I, madam, are in no respect on an equality, and even were I to be kept prisoner here, I would rather die than submit to this indignity." Let us think with pardonable pride of the brave Queen who could write so nobly under the oppression of her English jailors. De Silva visited Mary a short time after she wrote that letter, and this, in June, 1568, was the condition in which he found her: " The room she occupies is gloomy, being lighted only by one casement, latticed with iron bars. You go to it through three other rooms, which are guarded and occupied by hackbutters. In the last of the three, which forms the antechamber to the Queen's apartment, resides Lord Scrope, the governor of the Border districts. The Queen has only three of her women with her. Her servants and domestics sleep out of the Castle. The doors are not opened until ten o'clock in the morning. The Queen is allowed to go as far as the church in the town, but she is always accompanied by a hundred hackbutters. She requested Lord Scrope to send her a priest to say Mass. He answered, 'There are no priests in England'." Everybody knows there were all along plenty of papist priests, whose orders no one ever questioned.

In reading all this let us not forget that a year before, in the parish kirk of Stirling, the deeds which Mary had signed at Lochleven were publicly read, and the Earl of Morton took the coronation oath for the Prince and Steward of Scotland, the Bishop of Caithness anointed him, John Knox preached the sermon, and Mary's son was declared "Most excellent Prince and King of the realm". To an end then, on the 30th July, 1567, came the brave Queen's rule over Scotland. I feel compelled to confine this paper to a narrative of the heroic life and sufferings of Mary. I do not attempt a History of Scotland during Mary's reign. Elizabeth's treatment of Mary became now so bad that Mary had literally to beg. She wrote to her uncle, the Cardinal of Lorraine, saying, "For pity on your poor niece, send me some money. I have none wherewith to buy either food or clothes. The Queen of England has sent me a little linen and one dish; the rest I have borrowed. God will quickly me remove from these miseries, for I have suffered insults, calumnies, hunger, imprisonment, heat, cold; nevertheless, rest assured that I shall die a Catholic." Under the pretext of bringing Mary nearer to Elizabeth, Mary was removed to Bolton Castle, and a conference arranged to be held at York. Thither Mary sent as her Commissioners the Bishop of Ross, Lords Herries, Boyd, and Livingstone, Sir John Gordon of Lochinvar, and Sir James Cockburn. The Regent, of course, represented himself; he had with him Morton, the Bishop of Orkney, Lord Lindsay, and Robert Pitcairn; to assist in their deliberations, they had with them Secretary Lethington, Buchanan, Sir James Macgill, and the Clerk Register. On Queen Elizabeth's part there appeared the Duke of Norfolk, the Earl of Sussex, and Sir Ralph Sadler.

Mary had agreed to this conference without consulting her staunch friend, the Bishop of Ross; and he, on seeing the Queen, pointed out to her the errors made in agreeing to submission; but Mary believed in Elizabeth's professions of friendship, and trusted her blindly. She put much confidence also in the Duke of Norfolk, whose sister, Lady Scrope, had been to Mary a jailor of another sort than Dame Douglas. The Duke was at this date in his thirty-second year, in his third widowerhood, one of the noblest peers of England, a professor of the new faith, a messenger to York to do the bidding of his Queen. As president of the conference, he tried in the beginning of it to get admitted England's feudal rights over Scotland, but, failing in this, he set himself to convince the Regent and Lethington of the terrible injury they would bring on the Queen's cause, and that of her son, by seeking to defame her in the way they proposed. "If she is guilty, leave her to God, the only judge of princes. (There is a strong point in this advice, but, once the letters were cited, as evidence it was for Mary's interest to sift their value. She should, however, have tried to find means for doing so without compromising her dignity as a queen and the independence of her crown. The Scottish crown in antiquity was more venerable than that which came to Elizabeth from the Norman bastard and the lewd Catherine of France, who secretly espoused the Welsh adventurer, who metamorphosed his Celtic name into *Tudor*.) Destroy these letters, said the Duke, seek not to make her guilty, seek ye only that she ratify the abdication in favour of her son, and the confirmation of Earl Moray as Regent." Norfolk succeeded in this, but the Earl said, that for his own defence he would not destroy the letters. He had shown them to Parliament and to divers parties. The Duke, however, got him to promise not to use them. The extract from Mary's instructions to her Commissioners is enough to show Mary's sound common sense. " In case they allege that they have writings of mine which may infer presumptions against me, ye shall desire that the principal be produced, and that I myself may have inspection thereof, and make answer thereto." No other than the various forgeries were at York with the casket. These, with the famous forged warrant, signed, as Maitland and his associates declared, by the

Queen, were shown in private. Mary and Elizabeth both heard of the hole-and-corner way in which things were being managed at York, to the great displeasure of both, and Elizabeth demanded that the conference be held at Westminster. All the efforts of Moray and his set had failed to make impression of Mary's guilt on Elizabeth's Commissioners. " I see not," says one of them to Cecil, " how her Majesty, with honour and safety, can detain this Queen." But nothing could be done to induce Elizabeth to let Mary go. Mary's calm demand for a personal interview, the exposure of the forgers, and all their lying details, only did what was done in an earlier and sunnier land—harden the ruler's heart, so that she refused to let poor Mary go. The whole narrative, even at this date, makes every true Scotchman's blood boil.

## Chapter XVI.

### The End approaches.

>  Now blooms the lily by the bank,
>    The primrose down the brae;
>  The hawthorn's buddin' in the glen,
>    An' milk-white is the slae;
>  The meanest hind in fair Scotland
>    May rove thae sweets among,
>  But I, the Queen o' a' Scotland
>    Maun lie in prison strong.
>                    —Burns.

THE double-dealing and manœuvring at York were resumed and continued at Westminster and Hampton Court. Paris and Dalgleish were dead, and their share in the so-called discovery of the Casket and letters had the sanction only of what the conspirators said. Mary was not permitted to see the letters, nor to appear, but every effort was made to make the world believe that she was being found guilty. At the same time Maitland's scheming brain was occupied in endeavouring to bring about a marriage between Mary and the Duke of Norfolk, heedless of the facts that Bothwell had, by his help, managed, after a fashion, to become Mary's husband, and that that estimable nobleman still lived. The Queen was, for greater security, about this time removed to Tutbury, in Staffordshire. Elizabeth, finding out about Maitland's efforts in the Duke of Norfolk's interests, sent for the Duke to dinner, and jocularly remarked as he rose from table "to beware of the pillow on which he reposed his head". Leicester, who was sick, was then visited by Elizabeth, and she had no difficulty as she sat by the Earl's bedside in getting the whole story out of him. It is said that with many tearful utterances he craved his mistress to forgive him for having used his influence to marry her rival to one of her subjects. Elizabeth bestowed the solicited pardon; but to Mary she gave an additional jailor, so that she now had at Tutbury, in addition to the Earl of Shrewsbury, the Earl of Huntingdon; making her imprisonment most intolerable. Norfolk also got nine months' quarters in the Tower, and Elizabeth applied to Moray for further evidence against him.

This the Regent, of course, gave, and with the information he handed to Elizabeth a letter which he had received from Norfolk disclosing his intention of marrying the Scottish Queen. The English Catholics, while not openly taking up the cause of the captive Queen, issued, in November, 1569, a proclamation, declaring that they had taken up arms against the oppressors of the ancient nobility, and of the true religion, but no allusion was made to Mary's interests. In the north of England some 6000 to 8000 men were under arms. Cecil sent, under care of Sir Ralph Sadler, the Earl of Rutland, a boy of thirteen, to call out his tenantry. "Be tender and careful of him," said Elizabeth's Minister, "and, if negligent of resort to common prayer, admonish him."

At this point, another than the young Earl writes to Cecil about the watch on Mary while at Tutbury: "For God's sake, let her not remain where she is, for their great force is horsemen". As these horsemen were within a day's ride of Tutbury, Mary was, under a strong escort, taken to Coventry. On the 16th November, 1569, the rebellion broke out. Few of the higher Catholic nobles joined in it, and no foreign aid was given. On the field of battle no blood was shed; and no letters connecting or criminating Mary were found; yet orders were given to her keepers to shoot the Queen if an effort to escape was made, and Elizabeth ordered that such of the rebels as had neither "freeholds, copyholds, nor any substance of lands, be immediately hanged, and their bodies were not to be removed, but were to remain until they fall to pieces where they hang". The severity of Elizabeth's curative efforts may be judged from the fact that in the county of Durham alone there were 300 executions, and the High Sheriff of Yorkshire wrote to her Majesty that if he carried out her wishes "many places would be left naked of inhabitants". The leading rebels fled into Scotland, and afterwards escaped to the Continent. Instead of "fummellin' an' ficherin'" with Elizabeth and her ministers about her succession to the crown of England, Mary should have set about organising her partisans in England, as she had every right to do. She had, in fact, a better right than Elizabeth to do this. Then she ought to have roused the national spirit of the Scots. *This might* have united them, nothing else could. Elizabeth and Cecil certainly expected Mary to have done all this, for they were always suspecting her of it. In fact, it was the only chance. She might have failed, but it would have been better to die on the way to London than adopt the line she did. She had also many partisans in Ireland, and all the emigrants in France, Flanders, Spain, Germany, and Italy

—English, Scotch, and Irish—would have flocked home to her banner.

I do not mean to enlarge this condensed sketch by taking up in succession details of plots and conspiracies less or more in the interests of Mary. The forged letters had failed. Mary had not bent her knee to Elizabeth, and though John Knox had said "that foolish Scotland would not obey the word of God when He had delivered that vile woman into their hands," Mary still lived. On the 24th January, 1570, Elizabeth wrote to Moray stating that she was sending to him a trusty friend "who would communicate her resolves to him". On the very day before she wrote that letter, Moray lay dead in Linlithgow, from the effect of the bullet of one of the many Hamiltons whom he had wronged. In his prayer on the occasion Knox calls Queen Mary "that wretched woman, the mother of all mischief. O Lord, if Thy mercy prevent us not, we cannot escape just condemnation for that Scotland hath spared and England hath threatened the life of that most wicked woman. Oppose Thy power, O Lord, to the pride of that cruel murderer." And how did Mary take the word of the death of this man, stained with the blood of Riccio and of Darnley, the abettor of Bothwell, the betrayer of Norfolk, her own maligner? She had suffered most from his villainies, yet, tender and pious, she wept over the sudden and violent death which had overtaken him. It was only his own immediate adherents who mourned the loss of Moray. I do not think that his country or his sister had cause to grieve. In Scotland, the great bulk of the nobility and gentry were for the Queen, but the party of the Regent, after his death, was well kept together by Morton, Macgill, and Pitcairn. In England, Norfolk was assiduously cultivating his interests with Mary and her party.

The politico-Norfolk love-letters of the Queen are interesting reading, but we will not be tempted into quotation. This Norfolk transaction was a piece of manifest humbug, and naturally came to a bad end. None of the parties seem to have known precisely what they were at, except the wily ministers of Elizabeth, who, chuckling in their sleeves, saw the birds hop into the trap. Randolph was in Scotland again sowing mischief in the interests of Elizabeth. "All the honest men in England," said Melville, "were sorry at it, of which number there are as many within that country as in any other." Randolph's intrigues raised such indignation as forced him to flee to Berwick, where Sussex and Scrope, under pretence of keeping in check Elizabeth's own rebellious subjects, were really trying to ruin Mary's friends in Scotland. The watchful and wise Mary lost no time in writing to the King of France and describing to him that Elizabeth's operations were meant to defend and strengthen against me "these rebels of mine, and to oppress and ruin, as far as possible, my good and faithful subjects, under colour of recovering the English rebels who have fled to Scotland". In April, 1570, Sussex, with 7000 men, laid waste one part of Scotland, Sir John Foster another, and Lord Scrope, with 3000 men, a third part. Professing only a wish to punish English rebels, they managed to retreat and carry with them many cattle and much Scottish gear. "They did burn and spoil along the river Rule, and the water of Cale; they overthrew Fernichirst, they burned and spoiled along the Teviot on to Hawick, burned it, overthrew the tower of Branksome, the House of Bedrule, and diverse other notable towers and houses; Jedburgh and Kelso, and all along the river Rowbank, they spoiled and burned."

These events, the issue of the Bishop of Ross's "Defence of Queen Mary's Honour," and the publication against Elizabeth of the Bull of Pope Pius V., did not sweeten that estimable personage's usage of Queen Mary, or lessen the avidity with which her soldiery seemed to rush into Scotland on any pretence. Sir William Drury marched from Berwick to Linlithgow, and there made a fierce onslaught on Mary's unprepared adherents. Two of the residences of the Hamiltons were levelled to the ground, and Cecil boasted that that family "had never had such losses in all the wars betwixt England and Scotland these forty years". Lennox, the hereditary enemy of the Hamiltons, was with Drury, and by the help of Cecil now got himself elected Regent, and carried out to the letter the vindictive policy of Elizabeth. Sussex destroyed every Scottish castle and place of strength as far as Dumfries; Lennox with Morton did all the mischief that they could in the North against Mary's friends. On capturing the castle of Brechin, they hung thirty-four of its defenders. Mary's energetic appeals to the Kings of France and Spain induced Elizabeth to pause in her wild career. Perhaps the offer to Elizabeth of the hand of the Duke of Anjou, the favourite son of Catharine de Medici, had also a softening influence.

At anyrate, about August, 1570, it was rumoured that negotiations for the restoration of the Scottish Queen were on foot. The conclusion of the Westminster Conference had proven how groundless the charges against Mary were; yet Lord Keeper Bacon declared that rather than see Mary restored to her throne by the help of France, he would, with his own hand, cut her head off. It is not easy to know if this language was agreeable to Elizabeth, but this we do know, that Cecil and the others now made the reason for retaining Mary a prisoner, not that she had murdered Darnley, but that she encouraged rebellion in the north of England. However, the negotiations to restore Mary were pushed forward to please the Duke of Anjou, and Cecil was sent to Chatsworth to Mary. He was accompanied by Sir Walter Mildmay. "He and I," wrote Cecil, ' are sent to the Scottish Queen. God be our guide, for neither of us like the message." Cecil and the Chancellor reached Chatsworth in the beginning of October. They both seem to have felt Mary's power of fascination, and soon saw that three years' confinement and bad usage had not weakened her intellect or broken her independent spirit. On no account would Mary listen to Cecil's proposal that Elizabeth should get possession of the castles of Edinburgh and Dumbarton. He did not venture to try again to get accepted his treaty of Edinburgh, but contented himself with getting Mary's assent that her succession to the English throne was only barred in the event "of God not giving to her Majesty any issue of her body". The wise and witty Mary made the amendment, "any lawful issue," and the erudite statesman did as the Queen of Scots bade him, and added the words.

Other terms and conditions were settled at Chatsworth, and it looked as if Mary was to be restored to Scotland. Meanwhile Elizabeth was amusing herself with the Duke of Anjou, a lover young enough to be a son, whom at one time, "for her country's good," she would wed; at another, she would not; then she had doubts if so young a prince would be faithful to her; then, as if convinced he wouldn't, she, with an oath, declared that she would remain the maiden Queen. In Scotland, Mary's enemies, led on by the Regent Lennox, were wreaking their private vengeance all around, and Mary's heart was wrung by being told that Lennox was teaching her five years' old child to speak of her in the most odious and offensive terms. The sickness with which Mary was now seized, Fenelon said, "was more owing to this cruel blow to her affections, than to all her other troubles". Change of air was recommended, and she was taken to Sheffield Castle, where fourteen of her prison years of life were spent. After a long and severe illness Mary recovered, only to find the Chatsworth Treaty set aside, and three of her worst foes, the Earl of Morton, the Abbot of Dunfermline, and James Macgill, in London, with Elizabeth and Cecil—

> Abusin' hir, accusin' hir,
> With serpint wordis fell,
> Of reivers and rebeillis,
> Lyk hiddeous houndis of hell.

## Chapter XVII.

### The Troublous Pilgrimage Ends.

> My son, my son, may kinder stars
>   Upon thy fortune shine,
> And may these pleasures gild thy reign
>   That ne'er wad blink on mine.
> God keep thee frae thy mither's foes,
>   Or turn their hearts to thee,
> And when thou meetest thy mither's friend,
>   Remember him for me.
> —*Lament of Mary.*

NOTHING but evidence of cruellest injustice is to be met with by following Mary from prison to prison at the bidding of the fears of Elizabeth and her ministers. The record is a sickening one, and the story is humiliating to our national pride. Scotland's old chivalry had gone out with an evil odour like a tallow candle in the silver socket. We had a hundred harnessed warriors slaughtering a poor deformed Italian flute-player! For Randolph we had the canting Moray; for good Sir James, Morton; and

> For well-skilled Bruce to rule the fight,
> And cry St. Andrew and our right,

we had that cowardly pedant, "James the Sext". Yes, yes; it is well to abridge the record of the years that follow. They are but a repetition of the same story. By all laws, human and divine, Mary had every right to do whatever ingenuity could devise to effect her escape from England. She was held a captive against all law, and anything almost was justifiable that could set her free from the toils of Elizabeth and Cecil. Mary had little political knowledge or skill, she was always pardoning and trusting. Her reliance on Elizabeth's word passes everything in the way of credulity. She might have learned that neither Elizabeth nor Cecil could speak the truth, nor make a promise save to deceive. But her very innocence and trustfulness prove that she was the martyr for her faith which the Catholic Church has ever declared her to be; and which, Protestant as I am, from my soul I thoroughly believe she was. "There is a transparency in character which cannot be hid," and Mary was worshipped by her attendants and respected by her jailors during all the nineteen years of her "living death". Had she been a bad or an irreligious or even a careless woman, it is not according to nature that she could have concealed her real character for such a length of time; and that not even her enemies dare accuse her of other than the noblest demeanour during her captivity is triumphant evidence that in her Humanity had been blessed alike with a woman of sweet and gracious nature and with a Sovereign informed and resolved to do the right beyond most the world has seen. After years of manœuvring and all sorts of efforts on Elizabeth's part to get Mary taken out of the way, "without her knowing!" she, on the afternoon of the 2nd February, 1587, caused word to be written to the jailors of her captive that she did note in both of them "a lack of that care and zeal in her service that she looketh for at your hands, in that you have not in all this time of yourselves found out some way to shorten the life of the Queen". After causing this letter to be sent to Fotheringay, the pious Elizabeth waited for another five days, in the fruitless hope that, without committing herself, Mary's life might be taken. The hate of Elizabeth could not be infused into the minds of the jailors of the captive Queen, and so, on the 7th February, Mary's death warrant, signed by Elizabeth, was read to Mary. Then, in the hall of the castle of Fotheringay the next morning, about eight o'clock, the heroic and chastened spirit of Mary Stuart returned to its Creator. On the way to the scaffold, on seeing Sir Andrew Melvill in tears, she said, "Weep not, good Melvill, there is at present greater cause for rejoicing. Thou shalt this day see Mary Stuart delivered from all her cares, and such an end put to her tedious sufferings as she has long expected. Bear witness that I die constant in my religion; firm in my fidelity towards Scotland; and unchanged in my affection to France. Commend me to my son. Tell him I have done nothing injurious to his kingdom, to his honour, or to his rights; and God forgive all those who have thirsted, without cause, for my blood." Almost her last words were: "As Thy arms, O Jesus, were spread upon the cross, receive me, receive me, into Thy arms, oh, my God".

Incredible though it may seem, on the very day following, Elizabeth Tudor wrote to James Stuart, King of Scotland, only son of his martyred mother:

"My dear Brother,

I Would you kneW, though not felt, the extreme dolour that overWhelmeth my mind for that miserable accident Which, far contrary to my meaning, hath befallen!"

THE ABERDEEN UNIVERSITY PRESS.

www.ingramcontent.com/pod-product-compliance
Lightning Source LLC
Chambersburg PA
CBHW020241170426
43202CB00008B/184